Sources of Western Culture

| An Introduction |

LEE DONGCHOON / Brother ANTHONY

DAEGU UNIVERSITY PRESS

□ 저자 소개

이동춘

현 대구대학교 영어영문학과 교수
미국 로체스터대학교(University of Rochester) 영문학 석사, 박사
서강대학교 영문학 학사, 석사

Brother Anthony

Brother Anthony was born in England. He studied Medieval and Modern Languages and Literature at The Queen's College, Oxford University. He joined the Community of Taizé(France) in 1969 and came to Korea in 1980. He is Professor in the English Department of Sogang University, Seoul. His Korean name is An sonjae. He has published translations of works by many major modern Korean writers and is the author of two studies on Literature in English Society : *The Middle Ages and The Renaissance.*

1판1쇄 | 2011년 3월 10일
1판3쇄 | 2017년 8월 10일
지은이 | 이동춘, 안선재
펴낸이 | 홍덕률
펴낸곳 | 대구대학교출판부
경북 경산시 진량읍 대구대로 201
전화 053) 850-5661~2 | 팩스 053) 850-5669
http://press.daegu.ac.kr/
찍은곳 | 동아문화사
ISBN 978-89-7794-560-9-93840
정가 | 10,000원

· Contents

Table of Contents

Greek Mythology · 28

The History of Greece · 58

Apollo and Daphne by John William Waterhouse

Echo and Narcissus by John William Waterhouse

Pandora by Dante Gabriel Rossetti

Procession of the Trojan Horse into Troy by Giovanni Battista Tiepolo

Prometheus Bound by Jacob Jordaens

The Fall and Expulsion by Michelangelo

The Return of the Prodigal Son by Rembrandt Van Rijn

Introduction

History, theory, politics, economy, dialectic, democracy, tyrant, anarchy, alphabet, cosmos, tragedy and comedy, idea, philosophy, theology, geometry, atom, ode: when we realize that each of these words is Greek, borrowed directly into English, French and the other European languages, we may begin to sense what is special about a culture which is at the origin of so many different human activities that have continued from then until today. Out of Greece the modern world received both philosophy and science.

Rome, too, has left its mark in words: *republic, empire, urban, justice, dictator, liberty, university, humanity, religion,* and in whole languages too, since French (from which many current English words are derived), Italian, Spanish, Portuguese and Romanian derive directly from Latin.

The Bible continues to challenge and puzzle the world; the Christian faith has marked Western culture so deeply that it is still not easy to separate the two; yet why should texts, some written three thousand years ago, remain alive with meaning today? And not only texts, for millions of people look beyond the texts to the Living God and the Risen Christ in whom they find the origin and the goal of human history, at a time when there are more Christians in Latin America, Africa and Asia than in Europe and North America.

These great cultural streams combine fruitfully, but confusingly, to give Western culture: the *Graeco-Roman* and the *Judaeo-Christian* traditions. Put as simply as this, the reader may not realize the full scope of what is being said. The Jewish religion and people, the Christian religions in all their variety, all that has been thought and written in the Middle Ages, the Renaissance, the centuries since then until today in philosophy, poetry, fiction, drama, history, social theory, ideology, the Humanism which is at present fiercely contested in parts of the West, certain aspects of modern science, and much of the dialectics called Marxism, to say nothing of the art and the architectural design of many countries, all these have their historical roots here. What follows in this book is designed to introduce some of the main background to these.

This book tells briefly the history of Israel, Greece and Rome. It also tells about the myths and stories that originated in Greece, passed to Rome, and have come down through Western literature until the present day. One section offers an outline of the Christian Bible, with its many books written over nearly one thousand years, Old and New Testaments. It ends with a summary of the growth of Christianity, leading into the modern period. Many books exist about all those topics. We hope this book will make you want to read more.

Greek History

Greece stands at the gateway to Europe, whether you are coming from Turkey across the sea, or down along the north coast of the Black Sea. It is divided into two parts by the Gulf of Corinth, the southern part, the Peloponnese, being attached to the mainland by a narrow neck or isthmus, with the town of Corinth just to the south, and at the northern end Athens. The area around Athens is called Attica. In the Peloponnese, the central area is known as Arcadia and although it is really composed of very arid, barren hills, it has traditionally been represented as an idyllic area of "pastoral" living, the home of simple shepherds in a golden age of romance and poetry. Historically, the most important city in the Peloponnese was Sparta, the great rival of Athens and its opposite in so many ways.

Greece is a rocky, hilly land, not fertile except in the river valleys. The sea to the east is full of islands, the Cyclades, and the sea has always played a great role in the history of Greece. To the south lies the island of Crete, which saw the rise of a sophisticated culture (the "Minoan") before anything similar came to Greece. A related culture is found in Greece in the remains of the town of Mycenae, to the east of Corinth.

The highest mountain in Greece, Mount Olympus, lies in Macedonia, in the North East, and became the legendary home of the gods. Macedonia is the northernmost gateway to Greece. Alexander the Great was a Macedonian.

Between Europe and Asia Minor, separating the two, lie the Bosphorus and Dardanelles Straits, running from the Black Sea into the Mediterranean. On the northern shore lay the village of Byzantium that in late Roman times was to become Constantinople (now Istanbul), while at the westernmost end, to the south, lay Troy, the city of Priam in literature, to which Paris carried off the beautiful Helen. To the south of Troy, along the coast of what came to be called Ionia, the Ionian Greeks established cities, the most famous of which was Ephesus.

【Early Greek History】

In about 1950 B.C., bands of Indo-Europeans began to come into northern Greece, where they found people speaking a language similar to that spoken across the Middle East and living at quite a high cultural level. During the next four hundred years, they slowly spread down and took dominant positions in every local community they found, learning the culture, but introducing the language they had brought with them. This is the language that became Greek.

The Indo-European family/group of languages seems to have originated in the Northern plains, the Central Asian Steppes, among nomadic groups with no clear racial characteristic in common but with a male-centered culture that had learned to use the wheel and to herd cattle and sheep, moving pastures with the seasons. The spread of these groups occurs in waves, not as vast invasions by armies but as an infiltration of small family groups using various techniques when dealing with opposition. At times they would use force, at others they would make themselves welcome by peaceful means.

At about the same time as the Greek-speakers came down towards Greece, similar groups were spreading towards Italy, speaking what was to become Latin, and across to France and Britain where their Celtic language still survives in parts of Ireland, Wales, Scotland and Western France. Another group, also speaking the same kind of language, was descending towards India, speaking what is now called Sanskrit. By about 1600 B.C., these latter Aryans (meaning "noble people" although they were quite barbaric) were probably in India, where their literature and language are remarkably preserved in the "Upanishad" tradition, and the hymns of the Rigveda.

For the later Greeks, any language that was not Greek seemed rough and uncivilized; they called it "barbaric" to imitate the sounds they heard, the people speaking it are the original "barbarians". It certainly seems that the Indo-European form of language must have had some special quality, since it generally replaced the existing languages in areas penetrated by relatively small groups of settlers. There is simpler grammar, clearer structure...

【Crete】

In the centuries following 2000 B.C., Crete was exporting very beautiful pottery and jewels to Egypt and the Middle East, trade was the life of the culture and Crete had much experience of the sea. Then, in about 1480 B.C., the Eastern Mediterranean experienced a terrible disaster. A volcano on the Greek island of Thera collapsed, the sea poured in and there was an explosion probably greater than that of Krakatoa (A.D. 1883), so that tidal waves destroyed harbors and coastal towns everywhere in the eastern Mediterranean. The city of Cnossos, being away from the sea, escaped although it had suffered from earthquakes in the past. Yet a few years later, around 1400 B.C., Cnossos suddenly ceased to exist, the ruins show signs of fire and they seem to have been emptied of all precious things before being abandoned. What happened? Crete suddenly became a quite backward island, with only memories of its early cultural splendor

【Mycenae】

From about 1600, Cnossos was doing much trade with the mainland Greek city of Mycenae, which was in an important position on the route to the Isthmus from the Peloponnese. At this time, Mycenae suddenly learned many "Minoan" lessons, making pottery in Cretan style, making and using very elegant ornaments of gold and ivory, living in big, decorated houses, and burying its dead lords with fantastic treasures of gold which were found by Schliemann in the late 19th century.

Mycenae was not a Cretan colony, but a Greek city-state ruled over by a king, like others of the time, but it became a cultural center from which the products and styles of the Middle East spread into Europe. It is at this time that Stonehenge arose in England, and there are signs of contacts with Mycenaean culture there.

When Cnossos collapsed, Mycenae took over its commercial role and for the first time the dominant trading ships between the coasts of Lebanon and Egypt were Greek. At this time, the first Greek settlers (colons) seem to, have gone to live in Sicily and Southern Italy.

The society of Mycenae and the other rising cultural centers in Greece seems to have been patriarchal, feudal. Each local king lived in a palace at the center of which was a communal hall, *megaron*, with a pillared porch at one end, a fire-place for an open fire in the middle, and a bathroom near the entrance, so that the arriving guest could wash on entering (washing had religious meaning). Around the hall were the storage rooms, women's quarters etc. It is the kind of palace and the kind of society we find described in Homer's *Odyssey*.

By now the incoming "Hellenes"(the original name for these arriving Greek-speakers is lost, Homer calls the people living on the Greek mainland Achaioi) had introduced their various gods who, like themselves, lived in a male-dominated patriarchal village society located at or above the summit of Mount Olympus, under the less-than-perfect control of the main Father-god, Zeus the sky-lord, with his rainbow messenger and lightning weapon (thunder-bolt). This pantheon of different gods from different sources never really learned to live together, there were so many different stories about each one; at the same time the old matriarchal fertility religion continued as well, with its legends of Persephone, daughter of the Great Mother, carried down into the underworld by the god Hades for half of each year.

The quarreling, jealous, passionate gods of Olympus reflect the people of this period. Mycenae became rich, but after about 1200 life became almost impossible and the social system broke down. The main reason seems to have been war, not between nations but constant raids by land and sea, every lord and his followers trying to get more wealth by looting and stealing from those weaker. Piracy increased, so that sea-contact between Greece and the East stopped almost entirely for centuries, and Mycenae itself ceased to be an inhabited city.

It is just at this time, around 1200 B.C., and in just this society, that the events remembered in literary form in the great Greek legends of Thebes and of Troy must have happened. Agamemnon is shown as king of Mycenae or Argos, Menelaus as king of Sparta (then called Lakedaimon), there were other kings at this time in the cities of Athens (less important), and Boiotia. The stories in Homer and the great tragedies remember this age.

【The Dorians, Ionia and Homer】

Why, around 1200, do all the old, Mycenean cities cease to be inhabited? Where did the people go? Maybe fierce invaders, the Dorians, are to blame? Great poverty descended on Greece and many cities, like Mycenae itself, fell into ruins for ever, even the sites of some were forgotten. People left the mainland and went to settle on the west coast of Asia Minor, south of Troy. Here, in the region called Ionia, life continued for people from Attica and the Peleponnese (Athens was one of the only cities not to be conquered by the Dorians and therefore became so important later). In Ionia rose cities like Miletos and Ephesos, and it was for a time the center of Greek civilization. Early philosophy also developed here.

The Ionians, although now living in Asia Minor (now Turkey), thought of themselves as Greeks and remembered the stories of "life back home". They sang the old songs, repeated the old, heroic stories, learned the names of the old, dead kings. They also repeated the old stories of monsters and terrors to be met with in lonely islands by solitary travelers In 850 B.C., or maybe 700, nobody knows, these traditions became the source-material for two poems, the *Iliad* (the story of Ilion/Troy) and the *Odyssey* (the story of Odysseus / Ulysses) and the Greeks say that the author of these two epics was called Homer.

Nothing at all is known of him, seven cities in Ionia claimed him, perhaps Chios having the better claim. A little later, another poet of the same tradition wrote, in a Hymn to the Delian Apollo, "if anyone asks who is your favorite poet, say 'he is a blind man, and dwells in craggy Chios'." Since then, people have said that Homer was blind.

【The Iliad】

The name means "The Tale of Troy" (called Ilium/Ilion). Yet the main subject, Homer says, is the "Wrath of Achilles". The poem moves between the Achaian (Greek) army, led by Agamemnon, and the Trojan forces under Priam and his sons; it shows the sway of fortunes, and also the conflicts between the gods which influence events. But the greatness of the epic lies in its intense humanity. It is divided into 24 books. At the beginning, already many years have passed since the Greeks first arrived to attack Troy. Books 1-8 tell how Agamemnon, obliged to return to her father a girl he has captured, forces the Greeks to let him take from Achilles a Trojan girl he has taken. Achilles is offended and withdraws from the fighting, spending the days sitting in his tent with his friend Patroklos. The fighting continues, with attacks from both sides, and at the center of all stands the figure of Helen who comes down to see the battles from the walls of Troy, where the old men sit.

The *Iliad* describes many battles, and keeps including the varied responses of the gods who try to interfere in various ways. The theme of destiny is always present. One of the most touching scenes in the poem comes in Book 6 as Hector's wife Andromache urges him not to go out to fight, convinced that he is doomed to die, but he insists that as a warrior he has no choice. By the end of Book 8 the Greeks are in great disorder, many have died, they have been forced back and Zeus too seems to be their enemy.

In Book 9, Agamemnon calls an Assembly and accepts to apologize to Achilles and make amends, if only he will come back into the fighting. Only he can save them. Achilles rejects the offer, insisting that Agamemnon should be humiliated still more. He is wrong, but he persists. As a result, when the fighting resumes next day, the Trojans beat back the Greeks as far as the place where their ships lie on the shore, wounding Agamemnon, Odysseus, and many others. Zeus, meanwhile, has fallen asleep in Hera's arms (Book 14) and the gods sympathetic to the Greeks give what help they can, but when Zeus awakes (Book 15) he intervenes to give the Trojans the upper hand. In Book 16 Patroklos comes weeping to Achilles and begs to be allowed to go and help the Greeks. At that moment the Trojans set fire to one of the Greek ships, Achilles agrees and Patroklos leads out Achilles' Myrmidons, the Trojans are driven back. But Apollo disarms Patroklos and Hector kills him. Patroklos had been wearing Achilles own armor; this Hector strips off, and Trojans and Greeks fight for control of the body (Book 17).

Achilles hears news of his friend's death, and his mother, the sea-spirit Thetis, comes to comfort him. She tells him that if he kills Hector, he will also die soon after. He only demands new armor. Thetis goes to Olympus and asks Hephaestus to make it; meanwhile Achilles frightens back the Trojans merely by walking in their sight while Athena screams in support. While Achilles mourns his friend and washes his body, the shield is made in heaven, richly decorated and described at length. (Book 18) Achilles now enters the combat, and all must run or die. Even the river he fills with the dead; when the river itself attacks him, it is overcome (Book 21). All the Trojans take refuge in the city, only Hector stands at the gates, waiting for Achilles. Priam and his mother beg him to come in, in vain. The fight begins, at last the gods join in the fight, Hector is killed and Achilles drags his body round the walls of Troy, while his parents lament.

Achilles lays the body of Hector in the dust beside that of Patroklos, and they prepare the funeral of his friend. The Greeks prepare wood for the pyre, Achilles sacrifices animals and Trojan captives, and after Iris has summoned the winds, the pyre blazes all night. The next day there are funeral games (Book 23) The last stage (Book 24) involves the body of Hector, preserved by the gods. Priam goes alone, by night, to Achilles to beg for his son's body. He enters the Greek camp unseen, thanks to the help of the god Hermes. After a moment of high emotion, Achilles accepts Priam's ransom, has Hector's body washed and laid on the cart, then offers Priam hospitality. For ten days the fighting is suspended while the Trojans prepare the pyre, cremate the body, and bury Hector's ashes.

【The Odyssey】

The spirit of the Iliad is heroic, most of its action is violent fighting and slaughter. The Odyssey is quite different, full of marvels, journeys, and domestic household scenes. It is more "popular" than the Iliad, less "sublime". Like the Iliad, it begins in medias res (in the middle of things), but its structure is far more complex because of its use of "flash-back".

The beginning of the *Odyssey* is in Olympus, where the gods describe the situation of Ulysses/Odysseus kept prisoner for almost ten years after the fall of Troy on the island of the nymph Calypso while his wife and son wonder if he is alive or dead. Athena goes to his son, Telemachus, and orders him to go on a journey looking for news of his father. The house of Penelope in Ithaka is invaded by suitors wanting to become her husband. Telemachus sets out, and goes to visit Helen and Menelaus now reunited, to see if they have news. But nothing clear can be known.

Only in Book 5 does Hermes go to Calypso and order her to let Odysseus go. He makes a raft and sets out. He is almost shipwrecked on rocks but manages to land in an estuary. There he is found by the local princess Naussikaa, and brought to her home, the court of Alkinoos her father, who makes him welcome. During the evening he hears the minstrel sing a song of the wooden horse and the fall of Troy (Book 8) and he weeps.

Books 9-12 are the story of Odysseus's long journey from Troy to Calypso's island, told by him to Alkinoos: they avoid the dangers of the land of the Lotus-eaters and reach the Island of the one-eyed Cyclops Polyphemus, son of Poseidon. They enter the cave in which he pens his sheep, not realizing what a monster he is. Finding them there, he makes them his prisoners and begins to eat them. Fortunately, Odysseus sees a way of escape. First he prepares a sharp stake of wood, then he makes Polyphemus drunk with wine and blinds him. As they escape, the now blind Polyphemus asks his father to curse Odysseus and his companions. This curse is the explanation for all the disasters that befall Odysseus in his attempts to return home.

He continues with his tale, telling of the careless loss of the winds given by Aiolus, and the dangers of the witch Circe, able to turn men into swine, but who at last is forced to help Odysseus (Book 10); then comes the visit to the shades of the Underworld to consult the spirit of Tiresias on the way home. There he meets Agamemnon and hears of the way Clytemnestra and Aegisthus welcomed him on his return from Troy. He meets others of the dead, his mother too, from whom he learns that his father still lives (Book 11). Then they travel on past Scylla and Charybdis, past the Sirens whose song entices, and on to the island of the Sun whose cattle are sacred. There the sailors, hungry, kill the cattle. The ship is wrecked, all die, only Odysseus survives by his skill, and arrives at the island of Calypso.

Alkinoos equips him with a ship and the second half of the epic begins the story of the "Return of the Warrior", his arrival in Ithaka disguised with divine help (Book 13), finding hospitality in the home of the swineherd Eumaeus to whom he tells a false story of his identity.

Telemachus now (Book 14) returns from his journey, suspicious of the suitors who have laid a trap, while Odysseus makes the swineherd talk about his parents and the past memories of himself (Book 15).

In Book 16 Telemachus comes to Eumaeus' hut and Odysseus reveals his identity to him. Telemachus, then Odysseus, set out for the palace, Odysseus again disguised as a beggar. As Odysseus enters the courtyard, the old dog Argos recognizes his master, wags his tail and dies. The suitors welcome the old man with mockery, until he almost kills one. The tone now changes to foreboding as Odysseus observes them and plans his revenge (Book 18), while Penelope comes down into the hall and shows her faithfulness by her attitude. Later that evening, Penelope returns to the hall and talks with the old man, telling him of her ploy with the weaving done by day, undone by night (Book 19). Odysseus tells her a tale of an encounter with Odysseus. Penelope is deeply moved. He tells her that Odysseus will soon be back. His former nurse, Eurycleia, comes to wash his feet and recognizes the scar of an old wound on his leg; he forces her to keep the secret. Penelope tells him her plan to test the suitors with his bow and arrows.

The responses of people to the wretched-looking Odysseus show their moral character; bad people show no human pity for the unfortunate. The scenes of Book 20 stress this theme of judgment, of the difference between the cruel and the noble. In Book 21, Penelope fetches Odysseus' great bow, while he makes himself known to Eumaeus and the cowman Philoetius. The suitors try in vain to string the great bow, but get very angry when Odysseus asks to try too. Telemachus sends Penelope away, as the tension rises. Once all the women are away, and the doors bolted, Odysseus calmly strings the bow and shoots an arrow through the upright axes.

The slaughter of the suitors in Book 22 comes as a shock; it is a great conflict, not at all one-sided, although Athena's help is considerable. When all the suitors are dead, the women servants who have slept with them have to clear up the mess before being executed. The house has been purified. Meanwhile, Penelope has slept. In Book 23 Eurycleia wakes her and announces Odysseus' return. Penelope is too prudent to believe her tale at once. She goes down to the hall and sits in silence opposite Odysseus, examining him carefully. He arranges for music so that the families of the dead men will not suspect something. Finally, he realizes that she has been faithful to him during all these years and they embrace.

Book 24 (which many think was not written by Homer, but it is necessary to end the story) begins with the arrival of the souls of the suitors in the Underworld, where they are welcomed by that of Agamemnon, stressing the contrast between his return and that of Odysseus. Odysseus sets out to visit his father, Laertes, and finds him working in the orchard, dressed in rags. He pretends not to know who he is, and again tells of having met Odysseus some years before. Laertes shows his sorrow, and Odysseus identifies himself, proving his identity by remembering details from his childhood. Meanwhile the Assembly has met to discuss the deaths. The truth is told but the majority demand revenge and march out. At the farmhouse, the family and friends arm themselves with courage. Fighting begins, but is stopped by Athena. Zeus too intervenes to restore peace under the rule of Odysseus.

The Gods of Greece and Rome

The notion of 'god' is a complex one. What is meant by 'a god'? In modern English, a distinction of a kind is made between God, gods, spirits, ghosts, and demons, and much Judaeo-Christian influence can be felt. Many of the Indo-European peoples developed a rich tradition of epic, heroic tales in which more or less immortal figures play a role, often behaving very like ordinary mortal humans and becoming involved in human affairs. In the same stories we find a variety of nymphs and dryads that are clearly pantheistic nature spirits. The older stories about anthropomorphic gods very similar to people are reflected clearly in Homer's great epics.

Most of the gods from the Greek pantheon, and the stories about them (often called 'myths'), were adopted by Rome, whose language was Latin, very similar to Greek. Original Roman religion was essentially domestic and civic, with cults offered to spirits of the home, of storeroom and fireplace, (Lares and Penates) as well as to each family's ancestors. Often the Romans had perhaps retained the names of older divinities but not the stories related to them. This would explain why the Romans often had a different name for the Greek gods while telling the same stories about them.

In the following section, a few of the main characteristics of the most familiar gods are indicated. This was never a systematic religion; the same god had different characteristics in different stories or shrines. One attempt to systematize is reflected in the 'Olympian synthesis' by which several gods are said to be the children of a single father and mother, Kronos and Rhea. The Olympian gods then overthrow their father and take power in an epic war that serves to remind us that the Greek gods were not thought to be almighty or eternal. Immortality could not preserve them from loss of power and ultimate oblivion. The story may in part reflect the process by which the Indo-European pantheon replaced the gods worshiped in Greece before the Indo-European Greeks arrived; but it is also another example of the way in which the gods' experience of life is no different from than of humans. It is the awareness that the gods too are in the end limited that may explain the comic disrespect often found in Greek and Roman portrayals of them.

[Zeus] (Father Zeus)

(Jupiter, Jove in Latin)

Originally an Indo-European god (cf. Germanic Ziu who gave his name to Tuesday and Roman Ziu pater better known as Jupiter; the name is also found in India). At first a god of the sky, of the power of thunder, he later became a heavenly king, at which moment various other figures were grouped around him as a royal family and court, located on the Olympos (a pre-Greek word meaning 'mountain'). Homer gave this image such poetic force that the Greeks accepted it just as they were abolishing kingship in their own societies.

Since he very quickly represents the growing monotheistic vision,

Zeus is not usually involved in the ordinary things of life, but in the great issues, so that early Greek poets put Dike (personified Justice) at his side, and sees him as the protector of law and morality. The first writer of tragedy, Aeschylus, gives this its highest expression, making him a god of sublime righteousness and power. The Stoics used his name for the highest power in their system (fire which is reason), otherwise the philosophers tended to reject the name with the aspects of personified deity against which their systems rose.

【Hera】 (Juno in Latin)

Originally a goddess for married women. As the "wife" of Zeus, she is shown as the mother of Ares, Hebe, Hephaestus etc., and as the furious punisher of her husband's adventures with other females, divine or human. She is the enemy of Troy in Homer, and thus of the Trojan Aeneas in Virgil; but she is shown helping Jason. She was one of the three involved in the Judgment of Paris.

【Ares】 (Mars in Latin)

A god associated with the warrior spirit, unpopular and unloved in Greece, the second god in Rome after Jupiter! His character is shown as harsh, lawless, violent. Homer tells a story where he is the lover of Aphrodite, and not very clever, so that the other gods laugh at him when the crippled Hephaestus traps them together in bed with a magic net.

【Poseidon】 (Neptune in Latin)

Always associated with earthquakes and the sea, shown in art holding a trident, he is one of the sons of Kronos in Hesiod. He is also associated with horses, he is the father of Pegasus, the winged horse. He is also the father of monsters, including the one-eyed Polyphemus whom Odysseus blinds in the Odyssey, so that Poseidon becomes his great enemy for much of the story.

【Hephaestos】 (Vulcan in Latin)

Associated with fire, in Italy directly with volcanoes, in Homer he is shown as a smith, a craftsman and a magician, making Achilles' armor, the furniture in Olympos; he also made Pandora, the first woman, according to Hesiod. He was lame, but was very strong. There is a story of his being thrown out of heaven, which Milton uses early in Paradise Lost. He is shown, allegorically and humorously, as the husband of the beautiful Aphrodite.

【Aphrodite】 (Venus in Latin)

The goddess of love, in the sexual sense, associated with beauty and fertility; in art she is shown with majestic beauty in the fifth century, with charm in nude statues of the fourth. She was quickly used by poets to personify the powers of physical attraction, of sex. She is the mother of Aeneas by a human father, but Zeus tells her to keep out of the war. Stories about her marriage or (in Homer) affair with Ares also shows the ironic relationship felt to exist between love and war. She was awarded the prize in the Judgment of Paris. Shakespeare's Venus and Adonis tells the story of her love for Adonis, the beautiful young man killed by a boar. Originally this was probably a fertility myth, for Adon is Semitic for "Lord" (Hebrew "Adonai") and Aphrodite has connections with the Asian goddess Astarte.

【Eros】 (Cupid in Latin)

Originally, and until Homer, not a god but a word for passionate desire, usually sexual. He is clearly, from the beginning, an allegorical personification, and this explains why there are many different stories about his birth or origin. Hesiod, looking for a cosmic force, made him powerful over gods and men, dangerous as the one who "loosens the limbs and damages the mind". He is usually associated with Aphrodite. Since the lyric poets were concerned with the psychology of love, they show him as cunning, cruel, the cause of sudden madness; but he is also a most beautiful young man, surrounded by flowers. Sappho calls him "bitter-sweet".

The Hellenistic poets enjoyed playing with the lighter side of the love-experience; Euripides is the first to mention Eros's bow and arrows, but the later poets develop the picture, at the same time as they diminish his stature to that of a saucy, provocative, playful little boy with arrows of lead and gold. This is the picture that dominates Renaissance poetry, always as a personification of the irrational confusion that "falling in love" brings. Although Eros/love is said to be "blind", this is rather to be seen as a game, the child enjoys being blindfolded.

【Athena Parthenos】 (Minerva in Latin)

The patron goddess of Athens from ancient times, so that she is shown wearing armor of archaic form. She is celebrated as the patron of work, of skills, and so of wisdom. She has an owl beside her. In war she is nearly as powerful as Ares, but more committed because of her protective functions. Her temple in Athens on the Acropolis is called the Parthenon (Parthenos means Maiden). She is said in Hesiod to have sprung fully armed from the head of Zeus when Hephaestos split it with an ax.

【Apollo】 (Apollo Phoebus in Latin)

Honored everywhere in Greece, celebrated in the Homeric hymns. Always a prophetic god, especially associated with Delphi, he is shown in art as young and handsome, active in music, archery, medicine, law, justice, truth (so he is even said to be the father of Plato). His love for Cassandra, Priam's daughter, led him to give her the gift of prophecy, but when she then still refused his desires, he gave her the curse of never being believed when she spoke the truth. Someone who warns society of dangers and doom that people do not want to hear about, that person is still called a 'Cassandra'. Apollo is sometimes associated with the sun (Helios).

The Delphic Oracle was the most respected religious authority in Greece, but so often spoke with an ambiguous voice, that Apollo too seems a dangerous figure. The shrine at Delphi, at the foot of Mount Parnassus, was a place of sanctuary, and much treasure was also kept there. It was almost the only meeting-place for all the city-states. The oracles were given by a woman (Pythia) in a state of trance, and interpreted into messages by the priests. People coming with a question were obliged to be "pure", not only by washing and sacrifice, but in heart, too. As they entered the shrine, they saw the inscriptions "Know thyself" and "Nothing too much".

【Artemis】 (Diana in Latin)

Thought of as the daughter of Leto, with Apollo her brother, and the child of Zeus, she is mainly the goddess of all the wild forests and hills, a huntress, but also dangerous to women, causing them to die suddenly. But she was also a goddess of fertility, especially through the great temple at Ephesus that was her main shrine (Saint Paul had problems there in the Acts of the Apostles), and although she herself was a virgin goddess she helped women at childbirth.

She was often identified with the Titanesses Hecate and Selene, the former the goddess of magic spells and ghosts, the latter the Moon goddess (in Latin Luna).

【Demeter】 (Ceres in Latin)

The ancient mother-goddess of the harvests (giving corn for bread). Already in the Homeric Hymn to her, her companion-daughter Kore or Persephone, in Latin Proserpina, has been carried off as bride by Hades, the god of the dead, to his home in the underworld. Since Kore had eaten there, she could no longer escape completely, she therefore spent several months each year hidden beneath the earth. This story was celebrated at Eleusis, where the Mysteries taught very ancient fertility rites.

【Hades】

A son of Kronos, Hades was lord of the Lower World, to whose home the shades of the dead go; he is grim and pitiless. He was often called Pluto(n) (the Rich One) and thus confused with the son of Demeter, Plutus, the source of wealth. This wealth was originally a good harvest of corn, but the link with the underworld in later times extended his power to such things as gold and silver.

The Underworld is visited in classical literature by Odysseus in quest of Tiresias, Orpheus in quest of Euridice, by Heracles in quest of the dog Cerberus, by Aeneas in quest of his father. Virgil's Aeneid Book 6 gives the most detailed description of the geography of Hell. In the Plain of Asphodel, the ordinary "shades" wander pale. For the chosen few, there are the joys of the Elysian Fields, where they continue to enjoy activities they excelled at in life. Others, enemies of the gods, suffer the torments of Tartarus (transferred to the Christian world-view as Hell). Any soul arriving in Hades is ferried across the river Styx (or Acheron) by the boat-man Charon. A coin was placed in the mouth of a corpse before burial, with which to pay Charon. Those unburied may not pass, their spirits cannot rest. Cerberus the hell-hound is on guard to prevent any return. Phlegethon, the river of fire, flows there too, Cocytus, and Lethe, the river of oblivion, at which souls drink before going for reincarnation.

【Dionysus】

Worshiped in a quite different kind of religion, from Thrace, ecstatic, in which women (maenads) leave home and go dancing and singing through the hills, possessed by the spirit of the god, in a primitive frenzy (orgy) at the height of which they kill a beast or a child and devour it.

Another form, from Phrygia, gives Dionysus the name Bacchus, a god of vegetation, especially of fruit, and so of grapes and of wine. He was a sleep-in-winter, rise-in-springtime god, and in art he is shown surrounded by Satyrs and Sileni (young and old men, active passions, fertility). He was said to have been born from Zeus' thigh.

In Athens, the festivals of Dionysus (Dionysia) were the occasion for special songs and dances which developed into tragedy, first at the City Dionysia in Spring, to which people came from many parts of Greece, then at the Winter Dionysia, the Lenaea, when only Athenians attended. Dionysia then spread into many towns, giving them the occasion to stage their own dramatic performances.

【Pan】

Very familiar because of his flute, the Syrinx (pan-pipes), and his goat-like appearance, Pan became the symbolic wild spirit of uncontrolled Nature. He was able to inspire "panic" in sheep and humans, a sudden attack of irrational fear that sent them fleeing for no apparent reason. He was said to have appeared to the running messenger Philippides, as he brought news of the Persian arrival from Marathon to Athens.

【Titans】

The ancient poet Hesiod says that before the triumph of the Olympians led by Zeus, there was a race of Titans, the children of Gaea and Uranos, representing heaven and earth. Gaea emerges from Chaos, produces Uranos before uniting with him. The Titans include Hyperion and Phoebe, whose names are used to indicate sun and moon, as well as Rhea and Kronos, who are brother and sister but unite after Kronos has castrated his father Uranos and taken his place. Kronos was warned that he was fated to be overthrown by one of his children, so he swallowed them as they were born, only Zeus was hidden by his mother. Kronos later was forced to vomit up the others, there was a great war and the Titans were overthrown.

The most famous Titan (or son of Titan) is Prometheus, who seems to be a clever trickster in his actions. He is shown outwitting Zeus about the parts of the animal which men should keep in sacrifice, and the parts they should burn for Zeus (the men got the best meat, the gods got the bones and the fat). His most important action was the gift, or restoration, of fire to men. For this, says Aeschylus, he was chained by Zeus to a rock where an eagle ate up his liver for ever. In Aeschylus he becomes the model of defiance, the archetypal romantic hero. In most legends, Hercules rescued him.

Hesiod also tells how Zeus, to punish men for the sacrifice trick, asked Hephaestos to make the first woman, Pandora (= all gifts). Prometheus' brother, not seeing the risk, married her, after which she opened the "Pandora's box" she had been told not to touch, and all the evils of life flew out into the world, leaving only hope at the bottom.

【Personifications】

Greeks, and other Indo-European peoples too, liked to have personifications for all aspects of life. Among the main groups we find:

1) The Fates (in Hesiod named Clotho, Lachesis, Atropos) who spin, then cut, the thread of individual destiny.

2) The Graces who represent the charming qualities required in society. As three young sisters (Euphrosyne, Aglaia, Thalia) they are

often represented in paintings, standing naked together in harmony.

3) The Furies (The Erinyes or the Eumenides, the 'kind ones')who bring punishment on those who harm their family, who murder their own kin, who neglect sacred duties. They are vital in Aeschylus' Oresteia, where they are shown submitting to Athenian democratic justice, having pursued Orestes as far as Delphi (where those pursued could find shelter).

4) The Muses, from Hesiod onwards are pictured as the spirits of inspiration. He shows them living on Mount Helicon (his home) and bringing the poet theme and voice. On Helicon there was a temple to the Muses, and various springs there are famous for giving poetic inspiration: Hippocrene, Aganippe. Hesiod also gives the names of nine muses, later Roman writers gave them special functions: Calliope (epic), Clio (history), Euterpe (flutes), Melpomene (tragedy), Terpsichore (song and dance), Erato (lyric poetry), Polyhymnia (religious verse), Urania (astronomy), Thalia (comedy).

5) The Winds were personified as gods and worshiped by Greeks and Romans, together with other aspects of nature. Aeolus was the keeper of the Winds in general (whence the "aeolian harp" of Coleridge). Boreas the North wind and Zephyrus the West wind are already personified in Homer and these names are used in English poetry at least from Chaucer onwards.

6) The Dawn (Eos; in Latin Aurora, commonly used in English) is pictured by Homer in famous passages ("rosy fingered Dawn") as rising from her bed of love, drawing back her curtain, then leaving her lover Tithonus while she drives the sun chariot across the sky. The sun is also personified as Helios, Hyperion, Phoebus.

7) During sleep, Morpheus sends dreams about human figures. Night, too, is personified, as is Sleep itself.

8) Strife (Eris) is the bringer of discord; her most famous act is the origin of the Trojan War. By rolling the golden apple ("apple of discord") into the midst of the gods at the wedding of Peleus and Thetis, Eris provoked the quarrel that was settled by the Judgment of Paris, in thanks for which Aphrodite gave him Helen. Strife was also seen as the fundamental active principal in nature, dividing where Eros brought together.

9) The Horae are personifications of fundamental social ideals: Eunomia (Good Government), Dike (Justice), Eirene (Peace).

The word myth is one that requires careful definition. Specialists distinguish between different types of myth.

Cosmogonical myths explain how heaven and earth came into being. They are often the most important myths of a culture. The beings revealed in the myth, as well as the qualitative mode of creation, becomes a model for all other forms of creation in the culture. Sometimes a creating divinity will create ex nihilo (from out of nothing). In other cases, the ordered cosmos emerges, with or without a shaping agent, from a primordial chaos.

Eschatological myths are the opposite of cosmogonical myths. In eschatological myths, both death and the end of the world are explained and justified. An example can be found in Norse mythology: Ragnarok (Gotterdammerung, the twilight of the Gods). Here, the gods themselves are killed and the cosmos abolished.

Foundation myths Since the beginnings of cities sometime in the 4th and 3rd millennia B.C., some creation myths have recounted the founding of cities. Cities developed out of ceremonial centers, and those centers were seen as extraordinary manifestations of sacred power. This manifestation allowed for the expression of power in a specific place, emphasizing the value of sedentary human life. The myth of Gilgamesh in Babylon and that of Romulus and Remus in Rome are foundation myths. Other such myths tell of the origin of a ruling dynasty or particular tribe or nation; the stories of Tangun and of Park Hyok-Kose in Korea are example.

Theogenic myths tell how the gods came into existence. They are closely connected to cosmogenic myths. In Greek mythology, after the earth (Gaia) emerged from Chaos; she gave birth to the sea (Pontus) and the sky (Uranus). She and Uranus gave birth to the Titans, who in turn gave birth to the various gods and goddesses.

Transformation myths explain how certain mostly negative things came into this world. One of the most common transformation myths is that of the origin of death. In Greek mythology, Prometheus is blamed for this. He stole fire from heaven and gave it to mankind. In punishment for that, Zeus had Hephaestus make the first woman, the beautiful Pandora and gave her, with a box filled with misfortune, misery and despair, to Prometheus' brother Epimetheus. Despite all warnings, Pandora opened the box and since then humankind is plagued with all kinds of disaster, although hope remains. In the Bible, the story of Eve and the forbidden fruit has a similar origin.

Etiological myths are stories which provide a mythological explanation for peculiar things in nature or certain events and customs of which the origin has long been forgotten. Two examples are why the Ethiopians are brown colored (they were roasted by the sun when Phaeton lost control of the sun's chariot) and the story of why the rhinoceros has no hairs (it had been on fire once and then jumped into the water; since then his long hairs have never grown back). Such myths are primitive stories about the origins of things, symbolic and often anthropomorphic explanations of some aspect of the natural world that could not be explained "scientifically." Thunder is often explained as the voice of a god, and thunder-bolts (lightning) are shown as the weapons with which Zeus punishes and fights. Other well-known myths 'explain' what an echo is, or why the nightingale sings so sadly.

Fire theft myths are those stories, common in mythology, where a god or godlike being or a culture hero, a part often played by a trickster, steals fire from the gods and presents it to mankind. Fire was so essential and so mysterious that it was thought to have been at first the sole property of the gods. Since it was sacred, those who dared stealing it were often punished most direly. Prometheus stole fire in order to help humanity survive; in punishment, Zeus had him chained to a rock. Each day, a giant eagle swept down from the sky and tore out his liver, and each day the liver grew back.

Flood myths are the tales, found in many cultures, of great floods, often sent to rid the earth of humanity. The Sumerian flood myth is the oldest (about 2000 BC) and forms the foundation of the Gilgamesh epic. The main character is here Utnapishtim who builds an ark and thus survives the flood. In the Bible, there is of course the story of Noah, very similar to the earlier Sumerian myth. In Greek mythology, Deucalion is the hero of a very similar story. Survivors of such floods often became the progenitors of a new race of human beings.

Hero myths portray human figures of such heroic dimensions that they seem to be like gods. This is often expressed by giving them a god or supernatural figure as either father or mother. Thus Achilles is shown by Homer as being the son of the sea-nymph Thetis. Thetis was married to the mortal Peleus after the Titan Prometheus, liberated from his rocky prison, told Zeus (who desired her) that he would lose his throne to the son she would give him. Instead of a new Zeus, she bears Achilles and, in another famous tale, dips the child in the mythical underworld river Styx to make him invulnerable. Since she was holding his heel, the water could not touch it and in the end Achilles died by an arrow shot into his heel, proof that not even the gods can protect mortals from ultimate death.

[Hercules]

One of the most famous of all the heroes, Heracles (in Latin, Hercules) was said to be the son of Zeus and the human Alcmena, so that his life was cursed by Hera, the jealous wife of Zeus. Alcmena was the wife of Amphitryon and Zeus deceived her by taking the form of her husband and sleeping with her while the real Amphitryon was away at war. This story has been the subject of many comic dramas, until the present century.

Heracles/Hercules is best known for the "Twelve Labors" he was obliged to perform for King Eurystheus, a rather humorous story most fully told in a book written in the 1st or 2nd century A.D., although already familiar in classical Athens. Hercules' first labor was to kill the menacing Nemean Lion; Hercules strangled the creature and carried it back to Mycenae. The second task was to overcome the nineheaded snake known as the Hydra; Hercules' cousin Ioloas helped him out by burning the stumps of the heads after Hercules cut off the heads; since the ninth head was immortal, Hercules rolled a rock over it. The third task was to find the golden horned stag and bring it back alive; Hercules followed the stag around for one full year; he finally captured the stag and took it back alive. The fourth labor was to capture a wild boar that terrorized Mycenae's people; Hercules chased the boar up a mountain where the boar fell in to a snow drift, where Hercules subdued it.

The fifth task of Hercules was to clean the Augean stables, where thousands of cattle were housed, in a single day; Hercules diverted two rivers so that they would flow into the Augean stables. The sixth labor was to destroy the man Stymphalian birds; Hercules drove them out of their hiding places with a rattle and shot them with poison tipped arrows. The sixth task was for Hercules to capture a Cretan savage bull; Hercules wrestled it to the ground and took it back to King Eurystheus. The eighth labor was to capture the four man eating mares of Thrace; Hercules threw the master of the mares to them; the horses became very tame, so Hercules safely led them back to Mycenae.

Hercules' ninth labor was to obtain the girdle of the fierce Amazon warrior queen, Hippolyta; Hippolyta willingly gave her girdle to Hercules, but Juno convinced the Amazons that Hercules was trying to take Hippolyta from them, so they attacked him. Hercules fought them off and returned to his master with the girdle. The tenth labor was to capture the cattle of the monster, Geryon; Hercules killed Geryon, claimed the cattle, and took them back to the king. The eleventh task was to get the golden apples of the Hesperides; Hercules told Atlas (who carries the heavens on his back to prevent the sky falling on the earth) that if he would get the apples for him, he (Hercules) would hold the heavens for him; when Atlas returned from his task, Hercules tricked him into taking back the heavens.

The final labor of Hercules was to bring the three headed watchdog of the underworld, Cerberus, to the surface without using any weapons; Hercules seized two of Cerberus' heads and the dog gave in. Hercules took the dog to his master, who ordered him to take it back. Finally, after twelve years and twelve tasks, Hercules was a free man.

Hercules went to the town of Thebes and married Deianira. She bore him many children. Later on in their life, the male centaur, Nessus, abducted Deianira, but Hercules came to her rescue by shooting Nessus with a poison tipped arrow. The dying Nessus told Deianira to keep a portion of his blood to use as a love potion on Hercules if she felt that she was losing him to another woman. A couple of a months later, Deianira thought that another woman was coming between her and her husband, so Deianira washed one of Hercules' shirts in Nessus' blood and gave it to him to wear. Nessus had lied to her, for the blood really acted as a poison and almost killed Hercules. On his funeral pyre, the dying Hercules ascended to Olympus, where he was granted immortality and lived among the gods.

Of all his Labors, the most famous, because proverbial, is his cleansing of the Augean Stables, where the droppings of the suns a truly "Herculean task" (also proverbial). But he is first mentioned by Pindar in a more heroic style, killing two great snakes while still only a baby. In the tragic theater, Heracles is a figure of immense pathos, killing his wife and sons in a fit of madness according to Euripides, finally dying in torment because of Deianira's shirt according to Sophocles.

【Perseus & Theseus】

In a similar set of heroic tales, Perseus is born and lives surrounded by magic. His grandfather is warned (as in the Oedipus story) that his daughter's son will kill him. She, Danae, is therefore shut up in a tower so that no man can reach her. She is visited there by Zeus in the form of a shower of gold, a popular theme in Renaissance art, and a son is born, Perseus. Mother and child are thrown into the sea in a chest but survive, naturally. Perseus is mainly known as the killer of the Gorgon Medusa, whose hair is a mass of snakes and who could turn people to stone on sight. He is helped in this task by gifts from gods: Pluto gives him a helmet that makes him invisible, Hermes gives him wings to his feet, and Athene gives him a shield polished into a mirror (so that he can kill Medusa without looking directly at her). He uses the head of Medusa to overcome a variety of enemies by turning them to stone. He also saves the maiden Andromeda from being sacrificed to a dragon, and marries her. He finally kills his grandfather as had been foretold, striking him by accident with a discus during an athletics match.

Theseus was the great Athenian hero. His main exploits include the killing of the monstrous Minotaur in the Labyrinth built by Daedalus for king Minos in Crete. The Minotaur was the child of Minos' wife Pasiphae, who was inspired by Poseidon with a violent passion for a bull. Ariadne, daughter of Minos, falls in love with Theseus and with the help of a ball of thread she gives him he is able to find the way out of the Labyrinth. He forgets to change the color of the sails on the ship as he returns to Athens from Crete, so that his father Aegeus sees black sails and thinks that Theseus is dead; he kills himself by jumping into the "Aegean" Sea and Theseus becomes King of Athens.

In the story of *Seven against Thebes*, told in drama and forming the starting point for Sophocles' *Antigone*, Theseus has become the defender of human rights (as he is in Chaucer's *Knight's Tale*) and for Athens he was the father of democracy, resigning his kingship in order to unify the city. He is the symbol of Athenian mercy and hospitality in the tragedies of Oedipus and Heracles.

Theseus goes to conquer the Amazons, warrior-women, and brings one, Hippolyta, back to Athens to marry. This is the starting point of Shakespeare's *A Midsummer Night's Dream*. They had a son Hippolytus. Later Theseus marries Phaedra and her fatal passion for Hippolytus is the subject of Racine's great French tragedy *Phèdre*, inspired by Seneca's version of the story.

【The Trojan War】

Given the importance for Greece of the great epics Iliad and Odyssey, it is not surprising that there are many stories, found in various places, explaining the origins of the dispute between Troy and the Greeks. Helen's birth is told in a well-known story of Zeus uniting with a human woman. Helen's mother Leda was married to King Tyndareus of Sparta and they had a daughter Clytemnestra, but Helen was the result of a visit to Leda by Zeus disguised in the form of a swan. This is a scene much favored in Renaissance painting, and mentioned by poets including W. B. Yeats.

The other important background to the Trojan War depends on the link uniting Menelaus, the King of Sparta by his marriage to Helen, and his brother Agamemnon, King of Argos according to Aeschylus, king of Mycenae in Homer, to the clan of Tantalus. This is a family marked by some mysterious curse. Tantalus was at first a human who was a friend of the gods, in return for their favor he offered them his son Pelops cooked in a stew, trying to deceive them but of course, they knew what he has done, and brought Pelops back to life. The punishment of Tantalus is famous: he stands in Hades in a pond with water up to his chin and delicious fruit dangling before his eyes, but they "tantalizingly" withdraw from him every time he tries to drink or eat.

Pelops had two sons, Atreus and Thyestes. Thyestes seduced his brother's wife; Atreus, to punish him, gave him a meal of his own children, and he ate them, not knowing. Yet Atreus lived successfully, and died unpunished. His sons were Agamemnon and Menelaus, while the son of Thyestes was Aegisthus. For no clear reason (these things are not rational), all the curse fell upon Agamemnon, whose wife, Helen's sister Clytemnestra, took Aegisthus as her lover during the Trojan War. When Agamemnon returned, they killed him. Orestes and Electra, the children of Clytemnestra and Agamemnon, later kill their mother and her lover in revenge.

This theme of the curse on Tantalus' descendants is as important in explaining the origins of the war with Troy as that, lighter and more comic, of the judgment of Paris and its reward. Strife (Eris) is always the bringer of discord. By rolling a golden apple marked "For the fairest" into the midst of the gods at the wedding of Peleus and Thetis (Achilles' parents), to which she was not invited, Eris provoked a quarrel between Hera, Athene, and Aphrodite, who each claimed to be the most beautiful. They agreed it should be settled by the judgment of Paris, the most handsome man of the day. Oddly, Paris is shown working as a simple shepherd although he is one of the many sons of Priam, king of Troy. The goddesses each offer him bribes; Hera offers him greatness, Athene success in war, and Aphrodite the most beautiful woman in the world as wife. He gives the apple to Aphrodite. In thanks for which Aphrodite gave him Helen.

Unfortunately, she was already married to Menelaus, and he had become the king of Sparta, not a very impressive figure. All the kings of Greece had desired her and in the end the only way to avoid war between them was to give her to Menelaus. Stories tell that after Paris arrived in Sparta on a visit, Menelaus left on a journey, leaving him with Helen, and they duly left for Sparta together. All the kings of Greece had agreed to protect the union of Menelaus with Helen, which obliged them all to join in the expedition to Troy to bring her back. The expedition was led by Agamemnon. As the Greek fleet prepared to set out, the winds were against them until Calchas the seer told Agamemnon that he would have to sacrifice his daughter Iphigenia to Artemis in order to gain favorable winds. This story too is the subject of great dramas. In many version she is spirited away to Aulis where her brother Orestes later finds her.

Homer and Virgil wrote epics set during and after the Trojan War yet neither is the full "story of the war" and each should be seen as a work of narrative fiction in its own form, rather than as a bit of the "Troy story." The end of Troy, its capture thanks to the trick of the Wooden Horse, is always in the background. It is told in detail near the beginning of Virgil's *Aeneid.* Knowledge of what happens in the end casts a shadow of doom over any Trojan story, such as Chaucer's *Troilus and Criseyde.*

At the end of the *Iliad*, Achilles has killed Hector, the son of the Trojan King Priam, although he knows that he is destined to die soon after Hector. In the *Aeneid*, Virgil tells how Paris kills Achilles by an arrow that strikes him in the heel, the only weak spot in his body ("Achilles' Heel"). After Paris has been killed, the wooden horse is prepared to Odysseus' plans. The Greeks pretend to sail away and one soldier, Sinon, an expert liar, is left alone in the Greek camp. His lying tale that the horse is a pledge of divine protection sounds so convincing that the great horse full of Greeks is brought inside the walls of Troy. Sinon was to becomes a proverbial symbol of deceit. Only the Trojan priest Laocoon and his sons doubt, and they are destroyed by huge serpents from the sea (subject of a most famous sculpture). The Greeks emerge from inside the horse, open the gates to the main army that has now returned, and the city is taken in the night. Achilles' son, Pyrrhus, kills old Priam in front of his Queen, Hecuba.

Only Aeneas and his companions escape, and he becomes the father of the Roman people according to Virgil, for whom Rome was the new Troy. The Greeks were seen as treacherous, deceitful rascals in Rome. Euripides made a great tragedy from the story of the surviving Trojan Women, led by Hector's widow, Andromache. Her later fate is the theme of a tragedy by the French writer Racine. On returning from Troy, Agamemnon was killed by his wife Clytemnestra and her lover; he was duly avenged by Orestes and Electra, in a series of events shown by Aeschylus in the three tragedies composing the *Oresteia*. Ulysses/Odysseus wandered for ten more years before returning to his faithful wife Penelope (the *Odyssey*). Menelaus went home with Helen and we see them reunited in a strange kind of unheroic domesticity when, near the beginning of the *Odyssey*, Odysseus' son Telemachus goes traveling in search of news about his lost father.

【The Argonauts】

The Argonauts were the heroes who sailed with Jason on the Argo, in quest of the Golden Fleece. The Golden Fleece originated in the following fashion. Phryxus and Helle were the children of Athamus and the goddess Nephele. When Athamus remarried, the children's stepmother, Ino, became jealous of them and plotted to get rid of them. She arranged to have seed-corn roasted so that it would not sprout. When the crop failed, messengers were sent to consult the oracle at Delphi, and Ino persuaded the messengers to say that the oracle required the sacrifice of Phrixus to restore fertility to the fields. Before Phrixus could be sacrificed, however, Nephele sent a golden ram which carried both children off through the air. Helle fell into the Hellespont (which was named after her), but Phrixus arrived safely at Colchis, where he married the daughter of King Aeetes. Phrixus sacrificed the ram to Zeus, and gave its pelt (the Golden Fleece) to Aeetes. Aeetes placed the fleece in an oak tree, where it remained until Jason arrived to claim it.

Jason, the son of Aeson, was the leader of the Argonauts and the husband of Medea. Because of a prophecy that Jason would someday do him harm, King Pelias of Iolcos sent Jason on a seemingly impossible quest to bring the Golden Fleece back from distant Colchis. For the quest, Jason assembled a crew of heroes from all over Greece; Argos built for the heroes the largest ship ever constructed, the Argo.

According to Apollonius of Rhodes, 55 men accompanied Jason;

Apollodorus lists 43 men and one woman, and various numbers can be derived from other sources. The lists do not correspond very well, but the following are some of the more famous names mentioned: Orpheus (the greatest musician of the ancient world); Heracles; Hylas (Heracles' companion); Telamon (the father of Ajax); Peleus (the father of Achilles and the brother of Telamon); Argos (the builder of the Argo); Polydeuces and Castor (or Pollux and Castor known as the Dioscuri, they were the sons of Leda and Zeus, and the brothers of Helen of Troy); Meleager (who killed the Calydonian boar); Zetes and Calais (the Boreads); Theseus; Laertes (father of Odysseus); Autolycus (son of Hermes and a master thief); Atalanta (a great huntress who was the first to wound the Calydonian boar and was beloved by Meleager).

On the voyage to Colchis, in addition to other adventures, Jason and his crew of Argonauts became the first humans to pass through the Symplegades (the Clashing Rocks, they crash together when a ship tries to pass between them); they also freed Phineus from the curse of the Harpies. When they arrived at Colchis, King Aeetes demanded that Jason accomplish a series of tasks to get the Golden Fleece: he must yoke a team of fierce, fire-breathing oxen and plow a field with them; then he must sow the teeth of a dragon in the field, and deal with the warlike armored men who sprouted from these "seeds"; finally, he must brave the sleepless dragon who guarded the Fleece. Jason accomplished all these tasks with the help of Medea, Aeetes' daughter, who had fallen in love with him.

After obtaining the Golden Fleece, Jason and Medea fled from Colchis, pursued by King Aeetes' men. On their voyage back to Iolcos, they (like Odysseus) encountered the perils of the monster Scylla and the whirlpool Charybdis and the isle of the Sirens, as well as Talos the bronze guardian of Crete. In Iolcos, Medea contrived the murder of King Pelias, after which she and Jason fled to Corinth. In Corinth, after many years of marriage, Jason finally deserted Medea to marry King Creon's daughter; Medea wreaked a terrible vengeance, killing the bride and Creon, and even murdering her own children. She then escaped, leaving Jason to mourn his losses. Jason was killed years later when he was struck on the head by a timber from the Argo.

【From Ovid's Metamorphoses】

A large number of mythical stories of various origins were brought together in quasi-epic form by the Roman poet Ovid, whose Metamorphoses is the source of most western writers' knowledge of them. Shakespeare and other Renaissance poets were particularly fond of the work. Ovid uses the many myths of change and transformation to explore the nature of identity and the process of time. A number of these fables are very familiar; most of the stories that follow (taken from Bulfinch's *Mythology*) are found there.

【Daphne】

Daphne was Apollo's first love. It was not brought about by accident, but by the malice of Cupid (Eros). Apollo saw the boy playing with his bow and arrows; and said to him, "What have you to do with warlike weapons, saucy boy? Leave them for hands worthy of them." Venus's boy heard these words, and rejoined, "Your arrows may strike all things else, Apollo, but mine shall strike you." So saying, he took his stand on a rock of Parnassus, and drew from his quiver two arrows of different workmanship, one to excite love, the other to repel it. The former was of gold and sharp-pointed, the latter blunt and tipped with lead. With the leaden shaft he struck the nymph Daphne, the daughter of the river god Peneus, and with the golden one Apollo, through the heart.

At once the god was filled with love for the maiden, while she abhorred the thought of loving. Apollo loved her, and longed to obtain her; and he who gives oracles to all the world was not wise enough to look into his own fortunes. He followed her; she fled, swifter than the wind, and delayed not a moment at his entreaties. So flew the god and the virgin, he on the wings of love, and she on those of fear. The pursuer is the more rapid, however, and gains upon her, and his panting breath blows upon her hair.

Her strength begins to fail, and, ready to sink, she calls upon her father, the river god: "Help me, Peneus! open the earth to enclose me, or change my form, which has brought me into this danger!" Scarcely had she spoken, when a stiffness seized all her limbs; her bosom began to be enclosed in bark; her hair became leaves; her arms became branches; her foot stuck fast in the ground, as a root; her face became a tree-top retaining nothing of its former self but its beauty.

Apollo stood amazed. He touched the stem, and felt the flesh tremble under the new bark. He embraced the branches, and lavished kisses on the wood. The branches shrank from his lips. "Since you cannot be my wife," said he, "you shall assuredly be my tree. I will wear you for my crown; I will decorate with you my harp and my quiver; and when the great Roman conquerors lead up the triumphal pomp to the Capitol, you shall be woven into wreaths for their brows. And, as eternal youth is mine, you also shall be always green, and your leaf know no decay." The nymph, now changed into a Laurel tree, bowed its head in grateful acknowledgment.

【Deucalion】

Deucalion was the son of Prometheus and Clymene. When Zeus punished humankind for their lack of respect by sending a great flood, Deucalion and his wife Pyrrha were the sole survivors. They were saved because of their piety. Prometheus advised his son to build an ark and they survived by staying on the boat. When they were finally able to get back on land (on Mount Parnassos), they gave thank offerings to Zeus and consulted the oracle of Themis how they might replenish the earth with humans once again. They were told to throw the bones of their mother behind their shoulder and the human race would reappear. Since the mother of all is Earth, they threw stones and re-established the human race. The stones thrown by Pyrrha became women, those thrown by Deucalion became men. The son of Deucalion and Pyrrha was Hellen, who gave his name to the Greek people as a whole (Hellas is the Greek name for Greece).

【Pyramus and Thisbe】

Pyramus was the handsomest youth, and Thisbe the fairest maiden, in all Babylonia, where Semiramis reigned. Their parents occupied adjoining houses; acquaintance ripened into love. They would gladly have married, but their parents forbade it. One thing, however, they could not forbid that love should glow with equal ardor in the bosoms of both. They conversed by signs and glances, and the fire burned more intensely for being covered up.

In the wall that parted the two houses there was a crack, caused by some fault in the structure. No one had remarked it before, but the lovers discovered it. What will not love discover! It afforded a passage to the voice; and tender messages used to pass backward and forward through the gap. As they stood, Pyramus on this side, Thisbe on that, their breaths would mingle. "Cruel wall," they said, "why do you keep two lovers apart? But we will not be ungrateful. We owe you, we confess, the privilege of transmitting loving words to willing, ears." Such words they uttered on different sides of the wall; and when night came and they must say farewell, they pressed their lips upon the wall, she on her side, he on his, as they could come no nearer.

One morning, they met at the accustomed spot. Then, after lamenting their hard fate, they agreed that next night, when all was still, they would slip away from the watchful eyes, leave their dwellings and repair to a wellknown edifice outside the city called the Tomb of Ninus, and that the one who came first should await the other at the foot of a certain tree. It was a white mulberry tree, and stood near a cool spring. All was agreed on, and they waited impatiently for the sun to go down beneath the waters and night to rise up from them. Then cautiously Thisbe stole forth, unobserved by the family, her head covered with a veil, made her way to the monument and sat down under the tree. As she sat alone in the dim light of the evening she saw a lioness, her jaws bloodied with recent slaughter, approaching the fountain to slake her thirst. Thisbe fled at the sight, and sought refuge in the hollow of a rock. As she fled she dropped her veil. The lioness after drinking at the spring turned to retreat to the woods, and seeing the veil on the ground, tossed and rent it with her bloody mouth.

Pyramus, having been delayed, now approached the place of meeting. He saw in the sand the footsteps of the lion. Presently he found the veil all rent and bloody. He took up the veil, carried it with him to the appointed tree, and covered it with kisses and with tears. "My blood also shall stain your texture," said he, and drawing his sword plunged it into his heart. The blood spurted from the wound, and tinged the white mulberries of the tree all red; and sinking into the earth reached the roots, so that the red color mounted through the trunk to the fruit.

By this time Thisbe, still trembling with fear, stepped cautiously forth, looking anxiously for the youth, eager to tell him the danger she had escaped. When she came to the spot and saw the changed color of the mulberries she doubted whether it was the same place. While she hesitated she saw someone struggling in the agonies of death. She started back, but as soon as she recognized her lover, she screamed and beat her breast, embracing the lifeless body, pouring tears into its wounds, and imprinting kisses on the cold lips.

She saw her veil stained with blood and the scabbard empty of its sword. "Thy own hand has slain thee, for my sake," she said. "I too can be brave for once, and my love is as strong as thine. I will follow thee in death, for I have been the cause; and death which alone could part us shall not prevent my joining thee. And ye, unhappy parents of us both, deny us not our united request. As love and death have joined us, let one tomb contain us. And thou, tree, retain the marks of slaughter. Let thy berries still serve for memorials of our blood."

So saying she plunged the sword into her breast. Her parents ratified her wish, the gods also ratified it. The two bodies were buried in one sepulcher, and the tree ever after brought forth purple berries, as it does to this day.

【Echo and Narcissus】

Echo was a beautiful nymph, fond of the woods and hills but Echo had one failing; she was fond of talking, and whether always wanted the last word. One day Juno was seeking her husband, who was amusing himself among the nymphs. Echo by her talk contrived to detain the goddess till the nymphs made their escape. When Juno discovered it, she passed sentence upon Echo: "You shall forfeit the use of that tongue with which you have cheated me, except for that one purpose you are so fond of — reply. You shall still have the last word, but no power to speak first."

Echo saw Narcissus, a beautiful youth, as he was hunting in the mountains. She loved him and followed him. She longed to address him but it was not in her power. She waited with impatience for him to speak first, and had her answer ready. One day the youth, separated from his companions, shouted aloud, "Who's here?" Echo replied, "Here." Narcissus looked around, but seeing no one, called out, "Come." Echo answered, "Come," and hastened to the spot, ready to throw her arms about his neck. He started back, exclaiming, "Hands off! I would rather die than you should have me!" "Have me," said she; but it was all in vain.

From that time forth she lived in hiding. Her form faded with grief, till at last all her flesh shrank away. Her bones were changed into rocks and there was nothing left of her but her voice. With that she is still ready to reply to anyone who calls her, and keeps up her old habit of having the last word. Narcissus's cruelty in this case was not the only instance. He shunned all the rest of the nymphs, as he had done poor Echo. One day a maiden who had in vain endeavored to attract him uttered a prayer that he might some time or other feel what it was to love and meet no return of affection. The avenging goddess heard and granted the prayer.

There was a clear fountain, with water like silver. Hither came one day the youth, thirsty. He stooped down to drink, and saw his own image in the water; he thought it was some beautiful water-spirit living in the fountain. He stood gazing with admiration at those bright eyes, those locks curled like the locks of Bacchus or Apollo, the rounded cheeks, the ivory neck, the parted lips, and the glow of health and exercise over all. He fell in love with himself. He brought his lips near to take a kiss; he plunged his arms in to embrace the beloved object. It fled at the touch, but returned again after a moment and renewed the fascination. He could not tear himself away; he lost all thought of food or rest. while he hovered over the brink of the fountain gazing upon his own image.

He talked with the supposed spirit: "Why, beautiful being, do you shun me? Surely my face is not one to repel you. The nymphs love me, and you yourself look not indifferent upon me. When I stretch forth my arms you do the same; and you smile upon me." His tears fell into the water and disturbed the image. As he saw it depart, he exclaimed, "Stay, I entreat you! Let me at least gaze upon you, if I may not touch you." With this, and much more of the same kind, he cherished the flame that consumed him, so that by degrees be lost his color, his vigor, and beauty. He pined away and died; and when his shade passed the Stygian river, it leaned over the boat to catch a look of itself in the waters.

The nymphs mourned for him, especially the water and when they smote their breasts Echo smote hers also. They prepared a funeral pile and would have burned the body, but it was nowhere to be found; but in its place a flower, purple within, and surrounded with white leaves, which bears the name and preserves the memory of Narcissus.

【Icarus】

Icarus was the son of the inventor Daedalus and a slave named Naucrate. King Minos of Crete imprisoned Daedalus and Icarus in the Labyrinth to punish Daedalus for helping the hero Theseus to kill the monster called the Minotaur and to escape with Minos' daughter, Ariadne. Daedalus knew that Minos controlled any escape routes by land or sea, but Minos could not prevent an escape by flight. So Daedalus used his skills to build wings for himself and Icarus. He used wax and string to fasten feathers to reeds of varying lengths to imitate the curves of birds' wings.

When their wings were ready, Daedalus warned Icarus to fly at medium altitude. If he flew too high, the sun could melt the wax of his wings, and the sea could dampen the feathers if he flew too low.

Once they had escaped Crete, Icarus became exhilarated by flight.

Ignoring his father's warning, he flew higher and higher. The sun melted the wax holding his wings together, and the boy fell into the water and drowned.

Daedalus looked down to see feathers floating in the waves, and realized what had happened. He buried his son on an island which would be called Icaria, and the sea into which Icarus had fallen would ever after be called the Icarian Sea (between the Cyclades and Asia Minor).

【Pan and Syrinx】

There was a certain nymph, whose name was Syrinx, who was much beloved by the satyrs and spirits of the wood; but she would have none of them, but was a faithful worshiper of Diana (Artemis), and followed the chase. You would have thought it was Diana herself, had you seen her in her hunting dress, only that her bow was of horn and Diana's of silver. One day, as she was returning from the chase, Pan met her, told her just this, and added more of the same sort. She ran away, without stopping to hear his compliments, and he pursued till she came to the bank of the river, where be overtook her, and she had only time to call for help on her friends the water nymphs.

They heard and consented. Pan threw his arms around what he supposed to be the form of the nymph and found he embraced only a tuft of reeds! As he breathed a sigh, the air sounded through the reeds, and produced a plaintive melody. The god, charmed with the novelty and with the sweetness of the music, said, 'Thus, then, at least, you shall be mine.' And he took some of the reeds, and placing them together of unequal lengths, side by side, made an instrument which he called Syrinx, in honor of the nymph.

【Diana and Actaeon】

There was a valley thick enclosed with cypresses and pines, sacred to the huntress queen, Diana (Artemis). In the extremity of the valley was a cave. A fountain burst out from one side, whose open basin was bounded by a grassy rim. Here the virgin goddess of the woods used to come when weary with hunting and bathe her limbs in the sparkling water.

One day, while the goddess was bathing, quite naked, Actaeon came to the place, led thither by his destiny. As he presented himself at the entrance of the cave, the nymphs, seeing a man, screamed and rushed towards the goddess to hide her with their bodies, but she was taller than the rest and overtopped them all by a head. She dashed water into the face of the intruder, adding these words: "Now go and tell, if you can, that you have seen Diana naked."

Immediately a pair of branching stag's horns grew out of his head, his neck gained in length, his ears grew sharp-pointed, his hands became feet, his arms long legs, his body was covered with a hairy spotted hide. Fear took the place of his former boldness, and the hero fled. He could not but admire his own speed; but then he saw his horns in the water, "Ah, wretched me!" he would have said, but no sound followed the effort. He groaned, and tears flowed down the face which had taken the place of his own. Yet his consciousness remained. What shall he do?-go home to seek the palace, or lie hid in the woods? While he hesitated, his dogs saw him.

They rushed after him swifter than the wind. Over rocks cliffs, through mountain gorges he fled and they followed. Where he had often chased the stag and cheered on his pack, his pack now chased him, cheered on by his huntsmen. He longed to cry out, "I am Actaeon; recognize your master!" but the words came not at his will. The air resounded with the bark of the dogs. Presently one fastened on his back, another seized his shoulder. While they held their master, the rest of the pack came up and buried their teeth in his flesh.

His friends and fellow-huntmen cheered on the dogs, and looked everywhere for Actaeon calling on him to join the sport. At the sound of his name he turned his head, and heard them regret that he should be away. He earnestly wished he was. He would have been well pleased to see the exploits of his dogs, but to feel them was too much. They were all around him, rending and tearing; and it was not till they had torn his life out that the anger of Diana was satisfied.

【Pygmalion】

Pygmalion was a sculptor, and had made with wonderful skill a statue of ivory, so beautiful that no living woman came anywhere near it. It was indeed the perfect semblance of a maiden that seemed to be alive, and only prevented from moving by modesty. His art was so perfect that it concealed itself and its product looked like the workmanship of nature. Pygmalion admired his own work, and at last fell in love with the counterfeit creation. Oftentimes he laid his hand upon it as if to assure himself whether it were living or not, and could not even then believe that it was only ivory. He caressed it, and gave it presents such as young girls love, bright shells and polished stones, little birds and flowers of various hues, beads and amber. He put raiment on its limbs, and jewels on its fingers, and a necklace about its neck. To the ears he hung earrings, and strings of pearls upon the breast. Her dress became her, and she looked not less charming than when unattired. He laid her on a couch spread with cloths of Tyrian dye, and called her his wife, and put her head upon a pillow of the softest feathers, as if she could enjoy their softness.

The festival of Venus (Aphrodite) was at hand a festival celebrated with great pomp at Cyprus. Pygmalion stood before the altar and timidly said, "Ye gods, who can do all things, give me, I pray you, for my wife" he dared not say "my ivory virgin," but said instead "one like my ivory virgin." Venus knew the thought he would have uttered; and caused the flame on the altar to shoot up thrice in a fiery point into the air.

When he returned home, he went to see his statue, and leaning over the couch, gave a kiss to the mouth. It seemed to be warm. He pressed its lips again, he laid his hand upon the limbs; the ivory felt soft to his touch and yielded to his fingers like the wax of Hymettus. While he stands astonished and glad, though doubting, and fears he may be mistaken, again and again with a lover's ardor he touches the object of his hopes. It was indeed alive! The veins when pressed yielded to the finger and again resumed their roundness. Then at last the votary of Venus found words to thank the goddess, and pressed his lips upon lips as real as his own. The virgin felt the kisses and blushed, and opening her timid eyes to the light, fixed them at the same moment on her lover.

[Venus and Adonis]

Venus (Aphrodite), playing one day with her boy Cupid (Eros), wounded her bosom with one of his arrows. She beheld Adonis, and was captivated with him. Him she followed and bore him company. She who used to love to recline in the shade, now rambles through the woods and over the hills, dressed like the huntress Diana; and chases hares and stags, or other game that it is safe to hunt, but keeps clear of wolves and bears, reeking with slaughter. She charged Adonis, too, to beware of such dangerous animals.

Having given him this warning, she mounted her chariot drawn by swans, and drove away through the air. But Adonis was too noble to heed such counsels. The dogs had roused a wild boar from his lair, and the youth threw his spear and wounded the animal with sidelong stroke. The beast drew out the weapon with his jaws, and rushed after Adonis, who turned and ran; but the boar overtook him, buried his tusks in his side, and stretched him dying upon the plain.

Venus, in her swan-drawn chariot, had not yet reached Cyprus, when she heard coming up through mid-air the groans of her beloved, and turned back to earth. She saw from on high his lifeless body bathed in blood. She beat her breast and tore her hair. Reproaching the Fates, she said, "Yet theirs shall be but a partial triumph; memorials of my grief shall endure, and the spectacle of your death, my Adonis, and of my lamentation shall be annually renewed. Your blood shall be changed into a flower; that consolation none can envy me." Thus speaking, she sprinkled nectar on the blood; and there sprang up a flower of bloody hue. It is said the wind blows the blossoms open, and afterward blows the petals away; so it is called Anemone, or Wind Flower.

【Hero and Leander】

Leander was a youth of Abydos, a town of the Asian side of the Hellespont, the strait which separates Asia and Europe. On the opposite shore, in the town of Sestos, lived the maiden Hero, a priestess of Venus. Leander loved her, and used to swim the strait nightly to enjoy the company of his mistress, guided by a torch which she placed upon the tower for the purpose. But one night a tempest arose and the sea was rough; his strength failed, and he was drowned. The waves bore his body to the European shore, where Hero became aware of his death, and in her despair cast herself down from the tower into the sea and perished.

【Orpheus and Eurydice】

Orpheus was the son of Apollo and the Muse Calliope. He was presented by his father with a lyre and taught to play upon it, which he did to such perfection that nothing could withstand the charm of his music. Not only his fellow-mortals, but wild beasts were softened by his strains, and gathering round him laid by their fierceness, and stood entranced with his lay. The very trees and rocks were sensible to the charm. The former crowded round him and the latter relaxed somewhat of their hardness, softened by his notes.

Eurydice, shortly after her marriage, trod upon a snake in the grass, was bitten in the foot, and died. Orpheus sang his grief to all who breathed the upper air, both gods and men, and finding it all unavailing resolved to seek his wife in the regions of the dead (Hades). He descended by a cave situated on the side of the promontory of Taenarus and arrived at the Stygian realm. He passed through crowds of ghosts and presented himself before the throne of Pluto (Hades) and Proserpine (Persephone). Accompanying the words with the lyre, he sang.

As he sang, the very ghosts shed tears. Tantalus, in spite of his thirst, stopped for a moment his efforts for water, Ixion's wheel stood still, the vulture ceased to tear the giant's liver, the daughters of Danaus rested from their task of drawing water in a sieve, and Sisyphus sat on his rock to listen. Then for the first time, it is said, the cheeks of the Furies were wet with tears. Proserpine could not resist, and Pluto himself gave way. Eurydice was called. She came from among the new-arrived ghosts, limping with her wounded foot. Orpheus was permitted to take her away with him on one condition, that he should not turn around to look at her till they should have reached the upper air. Under this condition they proceeded on their way, he leading, she following, through passages dark and steep, in total silence, till they had nearly reached the outlet into the cheerful upper world, when Orpheus, in a moment of forgetfulness, to assure himself that she was still following, cast a glance behind him, when instantly she was borne away.

Stretching out their arms to embrace each other, they grasped only the air! Dying now a second time, "Farewell," she said, "a last farewell," and was hurried away, so fast that the sound hardly reached his ears.

Orpheus sang his complaints to the rocks and mountains, melting the hearts of tigers and moving the oaks from their stations. He held himself aloof from womankind, dwelling constantly on the recollection of his sad mischance. The Thracian maidens tried their best to captivate him, but he repulsed their advances. Finding him one day, excited by the rites of Bacchus (Dionysos), one of them exclaimed, "See yonder our despiser!" and threw at him her javelin. The weapon, as soon as it came within the sound of his lyre, fell harmless at his feet. So did also the stones that they threw at him. But the women raised a scream and drowned the voice of the music, and then the missiles reached him and soon were stained with his blood.

The maniacs tore him limb from limb, and threw his head and his lyre into the river Hebrus, down which they floated, murmuring sad music, to which the shores responded a plaintive symphony. The Muses gathered up the fragments of his body and buried them at Libethra, where the nightingale is said to sing over his grave more sweetly than in any other part of Greece. His lyre was placed by Jupiter among the stars (constellation of Lyra). His shade passed a second time to Tartarus where he sought out his Eurydice and embraced her with eager arms. They roam the happy fields together now, sometimes he leading, sometimes she; and Orpheus gazes as much as he will upon her, no longer incurring a penalty for a thoughtless glance.

In about 750 BC, settlers from the town of Chalkis on the large island of Euboia, north-east of Athens, set out to establish a trading base to the west, in Italy, in collaboration with other cities. They established the town of Cumae, not far from Naples. Not long before, the Greeks had learned the alphabet from the Phoenicians and the settlers from Chalkis took their form of it with them to Italy, where it became the Roman alphabet in which this book is written.

When the Greeks took the alphabet from the Semitic Phoenicians, they were taking a series of "pictograms", each letter being a simplified picture bearing the name of the object represented. The Greeks continued to use these names for the letters, although they did not know the meaning of the words and forgot that the letters were really pictures. "Alpha" (in Hebrew "Aleph", the Hebrew alphabet is based on the same tradition), our "A", is in fact the drawing of an ox, which is the meaning of "aleph". "Beta" ("Beth", as in the biblical place-name "Bethel", the "House of God") means a house, our "B" represents a house.

By a stroke of genius, the Greeks adapted some of the letters to represent vowels (A, E, I. O) while the Semitic alphabets only represented consonants. The Old Testament was originally written without vowels, the Jews only began to indicate vowels by a system of 'pointing' after

700 A.D. (the "Massoretic text"). A number of Greek letters, such as the well-known final "Omega" (its name simply means "Big O"), were invented separately.

One of the main Phoenician centers, not far from present-day Beirut, was the port-city of Byblos, which some Greeks thought to be the oldest city in the world. It was a major trading center and the Greeks gave its name to the "Papyrus" (= paper) made in Egypt from the stems of reeds, because it was often imported via Byblos, no doubt. Papyrus scrolls were the old form of book (in Greek biblion, plural biblia whence the word Bible = The (holy) books).

At about the same time, Phoenicians set up a trading center on the North African coast, the city of Carthage, which was to be a great rival with Rome in later centuries.

【Greek Colonies】

There was fierce competition between the Greeks and the Phoenicians although there were many more Greeks available. There were in fact more Greeks wanting to own land than there was land available in Greece, so that when the Cumae experiment was successful, every Greek polis started similar colonies, in Italy, in Sicily, and even as far as the southern coast of France, where what is now Marseilles began c. 600. In Sicily, settlers from Corinth took over the best harbor and founded Syracuse, later to be the greatest city of Greek Sicily and famous for its links with Plato.

Other settlers went in the opposite direction and founded Greek cities around the Black Sea and in the Middle East. Other Greeks went in search of trade with Egypt, before 700, and by their stories the cultural wonders of ancient Egypt became known in Greece, where they had an important influence on temple architecture and on sculpture, especially. At this time, Greece was beginning to discover the visual arts, particularly pottery, which it began to export.

Since Italy and Sicily are less mountainous than Greece, more fertile, the new colonies (settlements) soon became richer and bigger than the original founding cities, and could export grain back to Greece, which always needed it. Greek culture was strong enough to survive, especially since the original inhabitants of Italy had little of their own, and the settlers often made visits to Greece, especially for the festivals at Delphi and Olympia. This latter festival held in western Greece was originally in honor of the Great Goddess, but after being taken over by Olympian Zeus, the place was renamed Olympia. Legend says that the Olympic Games began in 776 B.C., but they are probably much older. Games were a form of sacred activity in Greek culture, a way of honoring the gods by human prowess.

【The City-State】

When Greek history (as opposed to legend and archeology) begins with the introduction of the Greek alphabet around 700 B.C., the population is divided between those living in towns, the city-states (polis), and those living out on farms some distance from the towns. Each city was surrounded by fields in the plain which supplied it with food; each city was tempted by the crops in the fields of other cities in times of famine or war, and raids were common, as were inter-city wars for other reasons. The towns were walled and sometimes, as in Athens, had a specially strong "upper city" Acropolis for ultimate defense. The feudal kings of Homer's heroic society disappeared during the difficult times and the government of the cities was in the hands of a Council of the "Best People", the aristoi (= aristocracy), who were from the important, noble families, those with most land and able to afford a horse and Armour to help defend the city in times of trouble. The Council of Athens (Boule) is better known under the name of the Areopagus, from the "Hill of Ares" where it usually met.

The Council would appoint executive officers, judges etc., at first for life, but later it was found better to change each year. There was also an Assembly (Ekklesia), composed of all the male citizens qualified to carry weapons, called usually to hear the decisions of the Council. Later, this Assembly became the main power in Athens, when Democracy was at its height. In the citadel of the upper town, where there had been a king's palace, they built a temple for the patron deity.

In Athens, at least, the old kings had proved helpless in times of war, so the nobles had elected a "General" (war-chief) to help. Then they also elected an Archon, or Regent, at first for life, to exercise most real power. The king (Basileos) remained with the sacred functions in-volving sacrifices etc. in the name of the city.

Even in democratic Athens, there was a person called "king" (the judge at the trial of Socrates had the title), but now chosen annually, together with the Archon, who ranked highest, and the War-Chief, who ranked third. In addition, later, they chose six judges because all the work was too much for the Archon, the chief judge, to do. The king was the judge in religious cases, including murder (the shedding of blood brought a curse, as at the beginning of Oedipus). Thus, Athens was finally governed by nine Archons.

At times of deep social discord, it became impossible for the citizens to agree, and the archon or archons could not be elected for the year. This is the origin of the word "anarchy" (no archon, no ruler, no law).

【Social Change】

With the explosion in international trade, new social classes grew up in the cities: ship-owners, manufacturers with 50-60 slaves, farmers. Around 625, the inhabitants of the city of Aigina became the first Europeans to use coined money, which they learned from the Lydians in Asia Minor. The result was a large increase in the number of rich people who wanted to be part of the aristocracies but who were often not admitted to the Council by the old families. Their other demand was for land, and this could not be solved by sending these people to Italy, as had been done previously.

The result was Revolution, with some high-born discontent leading the others in a rising, expelling the old powerful families and taking power for themselves. This power was then usually exercised in an autocratic way by the new leaders, who were known as tyrannoi, meaning "The Boss". The tyrant was usually at first highly popular, since he would distribute the land of the expelled families to his companions and build socially useful things such as aqueducts for water. He would then begin to act like a despot, surround himself with security guards, and finally be overthrown, although a few lasted as much as seventy years or more (Corinth). The result was much social unrest, as differences within society grew.

Sparta and Athens were now to arise as the major centers of Greek culture and power, their rivalry would dominate the next centuries.

【Sparta】

The Dorian city of Sparta, which came to dominate the cities of the Peloponnese, was an early center of refined culture but soon it became the dominant city over a wide rural area and the problem of keeping control arose. Under the "true Spartans" there were many "serfs" called helots, who farmed the land and also acted as foot-soldiers, while the Assembly of the city was made up of the men aged over 30 from only a small number of families. These high-class families were the only true "Spartans".

In order to keep control of this unstable situation (there were far more helots than Spartans), at some time before 600 B.C. the Spartan life-style was developed. Traditionally it is ascribed to Lycurgus. Basically it was a conservative, totalitarian socio-military system, which lasted for several centuries, under which the boys of the Spartan families were taken from their homes at the age of seven and put to "school" in packs until they were twenty. During this time they were trained in a very hard way, sleeping on rushes, wearing the same clothes winter and summer, eating rough food, learning to be total soldiers. At twenty they had to apply for membership of a group (15 soldiers in each), and from that time they lived together, even after marriage when they were thirty. Weak babies were exposed, girls also had a tough program of physical training, and the main activities of the men were military training, hunting, athletics. The only art forms that survived were the Dorian choral songs and dances, but they did not develop. Sparta for a long time refused to use money, and in theory all lived in complete equality.

The result of this was the finest army in Greece, but a life of total austerity, no individual freedom, and rigid, conservative, oligarchic government. Around 550-510 Sparta organized the "Peloponnesian League" of cities, a kind of "united states" in which independent cities undertook to unite their armies in times of war. This made Sparta the leading force in Greek affairs, also in the struggles against tyranny, and culminated in the victory against the Persians. The Peloponnesian War against Athens, first 460-446, then again 431-404, leading to the surrender of Athens in 404, weakened Greece and in the end led to its decline.

【Athens】

The area around Athens, Attica, was good farming land, and quite large, so that Athens did not establish colonies as other cities were obliged to do by their excess population. But by 600, the introduction of money and the international market economy had created a wide gap between rich and poor, with the rich selling grain abroad while the poorer citizens of Athens starved. The laws were no help; if you could not pay your debts, you and your family were sold as slaves by the creditor. The laws were known only to the high-class judges, whose sentences thus appeared arbitrary. About 624, Draco published the "Draconian" laws, under which death was the punishment for most crimes.

By 594, reform was urgent, and Solon introduced the first reform in Athens. He canceled all debts, had those who had been sold as slaves bought back by the city, forbade the export of agricultural products, and redefined the position of the Assembly (ekklesia), to which all free male citizens were to belong, even those without land. Athenian Democracy was essentially participatory, almost nothing important was decided by representatives.

Since participation in the Assembly took time, and was often boring, it soon became necessary to oblige people to take part. Security-guards went round the streets with ropes dipped in red paint stretched between them, directing the people towards the Agora (Market-place) where the meetings were held. In English, the expression "being roped in" still describes unwilling participation in some activity. Solon also reorganized the Athenian class-structure into four groups, according to income. Laws also were made more humane. The result was general discontent! Solon went traveling, after making the city swear to try his system for ten years.

From about 560 until 510, Athens was controlled by Pisistratos, who became tyrant in 546 after a surprise return from abroad. He ruled with Solon's constitution and was a popular figure. He died in 528 and was followed by his sons who degenerated into "tyrants" ruling by terror until Hippias was driven out in 510. During this time, Athens became a financial power, exporting the finest pottery, developing sculpture for the first time, gathering poets from other cities (Solon had been the first Attic poet) and growing into a rich, international city.

With the fall of the Pisistratids, their long-time rivals, the Alkmeonid family, returned in the person of Cleisthenes. The oracle at Delphi kept telling Sparta to "liberate Athens" (Cleisthenes had just spent much money rebuilding the temple at Delphi!) and after a bitter power struggle, in which Sparta was on the "wrong", conservative side, in 508 the people of Athens took to the streets in a two-day long uprising in favor of Cleisthenes and he introduced "democracy" in its full form in his reforms. Sparta tried once, the next year, to oppose him, but the citizen-soldiers of the other cities refused to fight.

At just the same time, in Rome, in a similar move, the citizens drove out the last king, Tarquin the Proud, and introduced a form of democracy, electing the first two consuls of the Roman Republic.

Cleisthenes created new divisions in Athenian society, no longer corresponding to wealth, or region, but uniting people of different origins, different social levels and different districts. These artificial units, called "tribes", had no real identity, so that the people would act in great unity. Each citizen lived in a neighborhood known as a demos and this decided which tribe he belonged to. Hence, the system is called democracy.

The administration of the city was spread among the people. Every day one citizen, never the same, held the keys and the seals, and with him sixteen others formed a team that stayed for twenty-four hours in the Round House, "presiding" over the administration of Athens. Each month (ten in a year) fifty Councillors belonging to one tribe (there were ten tribes) acted as daily "Presidents", the order each year decided by lot. These five hundred Councillors, different people each year, formed the second, "People's Council", which was responsible for the ordinary running of business. There were still nine archons each year, and they, if approved by the people, entered the Areopagus Council for life at the end of the year. The Generals, the war-leaders, were elected annually, one from each tribe, to command the regiment which each tribe provided from its members in time of war, under the War Archon, but they might be re-elected several years running.

【The Persians】

From 630 until 553, Persia was the home of a man called Zoroaster in Latin, originally Zarathustra, who became the founder of a new religion, full of this-worldly optimism, ethical, and sure of the triumph of good over evil after a great dualistic struggle. This new religious spirit gave confidence to the Persians in a new enterprise.

Beginning in 553, Cyrus set out from Persia to conquer an empire. In 547, he defeated the last king of Lydia (now Turkey), Croesus, who had asked the Delphic Oracle for advice and received the answer "If Croesus crosses the river Halys, he will destroy a mighty empire". Croesus, forgetting that his own empire was "mighty", duly crossed the river! In 546 Cyrus overthrew the Medes and took control of Babylonia and the whole of the Middle East.

In 536, he gave the exiled Jewish people in Babylon their freedom and helped them return to Jerusalem. There they rebuilt the Temple, which was rededicated in 516. Only later, around 445, did they rebuild the city walls. Almost two generations had lived and died away from the "Holy Land", yet they had forgotten nothing of their faith. This first Exile was a foretaste of the Diaspora that became total with the destruction of Jerusalem in A.D. 70, and has lasted until today.

In 529, Cyrus the Great was killed in battle, his son Cambyses succeeded him and conquered Egypt, where he set himself up as Pharaoh and, perhaps, went mad. He died in 522 and was followed by Darius who ruled until 485. Darius organized the administration of the Persian empire, centered at Persepolis, into twenty "satrapies" with governors, inspectors, taxes. His system lasted peacefully for some two hundred years. Darius mostly followed the new Zoroastrian religion. In 513, Darius set out to conquer Europe along the Danube, but the Scythians living there were too strong, he was almost overwhelmed and withdrew. It was just at this time that Athens was discovering the strengths of true democracy thanks to Cleisthenes.

In 490, the Persians first attacked Greece, landing their army at Marathon, on the coast North-East of Athens. Philippides ran with the message, and thus established the Marathon. The Spartans were in Sparta, and the Athenian army had to face the Persians without them. The Persians were defeated in a great victory which gave new courage to Athens. Darius died in 486 and was followed by his son Xerxes (born 519) who was to be the "great enemy" of Greece.

In 483, Xerxes began to prepare the conquest of Greece, letting his plans be well-known. Most of the smaller cities accepted his rule in advance. In 480, the great Persian army (200,000 men?) crossed the Dardanelles over floating bridges (taking a week) and advanced towards Greece, while other forces came along the coast in a great

Phoenician fleet. The Oracle at Delphi was not encouraging: "Either Sparta or a Spartan king must die."

Just when a great storm had destroyed many Persian ships, the Spartan king Leonidas with 300 of his Spartan elite confronted the Persians at the narrow pass of Thermopylai, blocking the way southward to Athens. But the Persians found another way round, and attacked from all sides. The Spartan king and all three hundred of his best men were killed in terrible fighting, in which two of Xerxes' brothers also died. Despite enormous odds the Spartans would neither surrender nor run away, so the Battle of Thermopylai has become the symbol of heroic courage, "the few against the many."

The Persians marched on to Athens, all the citizens of which had fled to the nearby island of Salamis. They captured the Acropolis, killed the soldiers defending it, and set it on fire.

【Victory at Salamis】

During the previous years, in the fierce struggles for influence that characterize Greek political life, one man had been rising in public view, Themistokles. In 483 Athens suddenly became very rich when a large vein of silver was discovered in the mines it owned. It was Themistokles, who foresaw already the Persian threat, who convinced the city to use this to build a new fleet of 100 war-ships in a new style, "triremes" with 200 men rowing 150 oars arranged in three tiers. When the Persians arrived, Athens had a total fleet of 200 triremes.

Although Xerxes announced the fall of Athens as a great victory, he had lost far too many ships through storms and attacks. Across the

Isthmus of Corinth a huge Peloponnesian army blocked the way south. The Athenian fleet was waiting behind the island of Salamis, ready to attack the Persians if they tried to carry forces across to the South by sea. Then Themistokles sent a secret message to Xerxes, suggesting that the Greeks were not able to resist, that they were ready to run away, and that he himself was ready to support Xerxes. It was a trick and Xerxes fell for it.

Less than ten years later, the story of that day was told in the only Greek tragedy to deal with "modern" history, The Persians, written by a man who had been part of the Athenian army that day, Aeschylus, and watched by the people of Athens who had been waiting on the shores. The Greeks defeated the Persians at sea, soon news of other victories came, and Xerxes sailed away, never to return. Greece, in particular Athens, was left to develop in its own way. The years between the Battle of Salamis in the autumn of 480 and the death of Alexander the Great in 323 in Babylon were decisive for the future of Western civilization.

Tell them in Lakedaimon, passer-by:
Carrying out their orders, here we lie.

That is the epitaph composed for the memorial of Leonidas' Three Hundred heroes who died and were buried at Thermopylae (the tomb mound is still there), a simple phrase designed to be cut in stone ("lapidary"), noble in spirit, a condensed "epigram" (meaning an "inscription"). Such epigrams were first developed at this time, they gradually became more complex, and separated from tombstones to become one of the basic features of lyric poetry.

When the Persians destroyed the temples on the Acropolis, there were already many sculptures there. In the rebuilding, these were thrown away, buried for centuries. They were "archaic" in style, stylized figures, not naturalistic, not idealizing, and most of the faces show a strange smile. The statues that were made in the period of the rebuilding are Classical, noble and, above all, serious. The twentieth century has rediscovered the charm of the archaic, but most people who visit the Louvre still admire the "Venus de Milo" as the model of classical" beauty.

【Greek Tragedy】

At the same time as Greek thought was developing in Ionia and Italy, in the 6th century B.C. Athens gave birth to tragedy and comedy. There seems no doubt that the rise of tragedy in Athens is linked to the growth of the two great Dionysia (festivals of the god Dionysius) : the City Dionysia in January and the Lenaea in March-April. Legend says that around 540 an actor, Thespis, introduced the role of a single actor (called "*Hypocrite*" or "explainer") into celebrations originally consisting of lyrics sung by a dancing Chorus of citizens. There is no clear solution to the question why this serious form of drama is called "Goat-song" (*Tragodia*) although it may be because the Chorus used to be dressed as Satyrs with goats' ears. Originally the choral lyrics must have celebrated the god Dionysius but already before Aeschylus, probably, other stories were being recalled. For the Dionysia, three writers were chosen by the city authorities and each had to prepare the texts of a trilogy of tragedies and a fourth "satyr-play". A prize was awarded to the best. The authorities also named a rich citizen to be the "*Choregus*" of each writer, whose role was to pay the citizens forming the Chorus and also cover the costs of staging.

Aeschylus liked to offer trilogies telling related stories, his *Oresteia is* the only surviving example. Others seem not to have followed him. It was Aeschylus who introduced the second individual actor, which makes dialogue possible. Sophocles then introduced a third actor and Aeschylus quickly followed his example. Sophocles also introduced painted scenery, which Aeschylus adopted too. While the Chorus was always composed of citizens, the actors were professionals, like Sophocles. The main actor was called the Protagonist. In the theaters of Greece, the play was a religious celebration, and therefore open to all citizens, free. Much debate has raged as to whether women were present at performances; modern opinion tends to think that they were. The statue of Dionysius presided over the performances from the front seats. The actors were masked, so that one actor might play several; roles. The steps on which the audience sat usually follow the curve of a hillside, around the circular dance-area on which the Chorus performed, the *Orchestra.* At the back of the Orchestra was the *Skene,* a wall against which there may have been a platform (stage) and with doors that could open to reveal the result of scenes of horror that happened out of sight inside. There were also machines to allow gods to descend from above. In Greek tragedy, violent actions are described, not presented onstage. The play is a series of lyric passages sung by the Chorus, interspersed by dialogues between actors or between actor and Chorus.

Aristotle's definition of Tragedy in the "Poetics" is famous,

Tragedy is an imitation *(mimesis)* of an action that is serious, complete, and of a certain magnitude; in language embellished with each kind of artistic ornament, the several kinds being found in separate parts of the play; in the form of action, not of narrative; through pity and fear effecting the proper purgation *(catharsis)* of these emotions. By "language embellished," I mean language into which rhythm, "harmony," and song enter. By "the several kinds in separate parts," I mean, that some parts are rendered through the medium of verse alone, others again with the aid of song.

Now as tragic imitation implies persons acting, it necessarily follows, in the first place, that Spectacular equipment will be a part of Tragedy. Next, Song and Diction, for these are the medium of imitation. By "Diction" I mean the mere metrical arrangement of the words: as for "Song," it is a term whose sense every one understands. Again, Tragedy is the imitation of an action; and an action implies personal agents, who necessarily possess certain distinctive qualities both of character and thought; for it is by these that we qualify actions themselves, and these-thought and character-are the two natural causes from which actions spring, and on actions again all success or failure depends. Hence the plot is the imitation of the Action, for by Plot I here mean the arrangement of the incidents. By Character I mean that in virtue of which we ascribe certain qualities to the agents...

Most important of all is the structure of the incidents. For Tragedy is an imitation, not of men, but of an action and of life, and life consists in action, and its end is a mode of action, not a quality.

But he was writing when all the great tragedies had already been written and the tragedians were dead. His words had no effect on the way they wrote and may very well not represent accurately what they intended to represent in their plays, which are mostly illustrations of the arbitrary ways in which Fate or the gods bring humans to suffering and disaster for no clear fault of their own.

Greek tragedy is not a 'morality play' in which people are punished for sin. Much depends on some kind of flaw or latent characteristic of the main character but all the tragedians stress the theme of blindness; humans cannot know that they are doing is a transgression of law, but that does not protect them from the consequences. There are a number of Greek tragedies which do not end with the death of the main character, unlike Shakespearean tragedy, for example.

"Song," it is a term whose sense every one understands. Again, Tragedy is the imitation of an action; and an action implies personal agents, who necessarily possess certain distinctive qualities both of character and thought; for it is by these that we qualify actions themselves, and these-thought and character-are the two natural causes from which actions spring, and on actions again all success or failure depends. Hence the plot is the imitation of the Action, for by Plot I here mean the arrangement of the incidents. By Character I mean that in virtue of which we ascribe certain qualities to the agents...

Most important of all is the structure of the incidents. For Tragedy is an imitation, not of men, but of an action and of life, and life consists in action, and its end is a mode of action, not a quality.

But he was writing when all the great tragedies had already been written and the tragedians were dead. His words had no effect on the way they wrote and may very well not represent accurately what they intended to represent in their plays, which are mostly illustrations of the arbitrary ways in which Fate or the gods bring humans to suffering and disaster for no clear fault of their own.

Greek tragedy is not a 'morality play' in which people are punished for sin. Much depends on some kind of flaw or latent characteristic of the main character but all the tragedians stress the theme of blindness; humans cannot know that they are doing is a transgression of law, but that does not protect them from the consequences. There are a number of Greek tragedies which do not end with the death of the main character, unlike Shakespearean tragedy, for example.

【Aeschylus】

Born 525, died 456, he is the father of Greek tragedy. He wrote some 90 plays, of which 7 survive: "The Suppliants", "The Persians", "Seven against Thebes", "Prometheus Bound" and the "Oresteia" trilogy composed of "Agamemnon", "The Coephori", "The Eumenides". The action of his plays is usually quite static, the tone, especially of the choral lyrics, is solemn, exalted and religious. He struggles to combine a respect for the gods, especially for Zeus, with the highest vision of human morality. The *Oresteia* leads from the news of the fall of Troy, through Agamemnon's murder by Clytemnestra to her murder by Orestes, encouraged by his sister Electra. Orestes is then pursued by the Furies for having shed his mother's blood, but is sent to Athens where he presents his defense to the citizens who justify him and dismiss the Furies' claims. The Chorus, old men of Argos, witness the events they cannot control, and pay homage to the greatness of Zeus.

【Sophocles】

Born in 496, died in 406, Sophocles wrote some 120 plays, won the first prize 18 times, 7 of his plays survive: "Antigone", "Oedipus", "Electra", "Ajax", "Trachiniae" (The Death of Heracles), "Philoctetes", and "Oedipus at Colonus". While Aeschylus is deeply religious, Sophocles shows a human individual at the center, choosing to act, then assuming the consequences of that choice. The role of the Chorus is less developed than in Aeschylus, while the dialogue in Sophocles is more 'realistic' and 'psychological' than in Aeschylus; the plays offer more detailed psychology, although always of a heroic kind. Antigone and Electra are noble female figures, gentle and full of courage. Sophocles' dramas have great simplicity, all is reduced to its noblest human essence. He was much admired by Racine, by Lessing; Shelley drowned with a book of his works in his pocket. He is the most frequently acted of the three in modern times.

【Euripides】

Born in Salamis in 480 (perhaps on the day of the victory), died in Macedonia in 406, Euripides was controversial in his time.

He wrote some 90 plays, of which 18 survive: "Alcestis", "Medea", "Hippolytus", "The Trojan Women", "Helen", "Orestes", "Iphigenia at Aulis", "The Bacchae", "Andromache", "The Children of Heracles", "Hecuba", "The Suppliants", "Electra", "The Madness of Heracles", "Iphigenia in Tauris", "Ion", "Phoenissae"... In almost all these plays the characters are shown in situations of great stress and conflict, torn by passions and affection. Euripides challenges traditional ideas about gods and morality. Heroism and beauty are admired; many of his finest characters are women. His plots favour surprise revelations, the Chorus has little contact with the action. He is the dramatist who comes closest to the emotions of "ordinary life" and for Milton, he is the messenger of human liberty

【From 480 until the Fall of Athens】

The great tragedian Aeschylus died in Sicily in 456. He had gone there partly to escape the quarrels that were spreading in Athens and across Greece. Athens had just completed the democratization of its government. He left his own epitaph, although it suggests that he did not think that his plays were so important, as they are not mentioned.

Here Aeschylus, son of Euphorion, bred
in Athens, lies in Gela's cornland dead.
His fighting prowess Marathon could show
and long-haired Medes (Persians), who had good cause to know.

Pericles was neither a poet nor a thinker, yet he was the central figure of Athen's greatest moments. Born into a wealthy family, in 472, when only 21, he was the choregos (sponsor) for Aeschylus' The Persians, which gained the first prize. It was designed to remind the divided Athenians of the great things they had done when they were united in 480. Pericles was the pupil and friend of Anaxagoras (the first philosopher to live in Athens), of Phidias the sculptor, and of Sophocles.

He was from a "high" family, but he was a convinced democrat, and he played such an important role in Athens that this is called "The Age of Pericles", not by being a kind of dictator, but by being trusted by the people. When he spoke, people listened to him, then they voted in support of his proposals. The Assembly of Citizens (*ekklesia*) was the effective parliament and Pericles had the right to address them in just the same way as even the poorest Athenian. Only he spoke so well that he usually convinced them, for his only power lay in the power of his oratory and he was one of the great orators.

This century is one of the glories of human history, yet it is a tragic story. While rivalry and war divided the cities of Greece, Athens was rebuilding what the Persians had destroyed. At the same time, it had much trouble keeping the Spartans from attacking. In 445 the two great cities signed a 30-year peace treaty, under Pericles' urging. From 454 until his death in 429, the Athenians chose him as one of the Generals almost every year, in peace and in war, and in 447 he was put in charge of the rebuilding of the Parthenon (House of the Maiden, Athena) and the other great structures still standing (in ruins) on the Acropolis.

When the people of Athens returned to the ruined city in 480, a young boy of fifteen had led the singing of the victory-song (Paean) in the celebrations. His name was Sophocles, and in 468 his tragedy was judged better than that of Aeschylus and won the first prize that year. Aeschylus, Sophocles, Euripides all wrote for the Athens of Pericles.

Plutarch the Hellenistic historian, writing in the first century AD, wrote of Pericles's age: "Buildings which men thought would hardly be finished in several succeeding generations were all completed within the political prime of one man... Generally, facility and speed are not conducive to lasting impressiveness and the highest beauty; the time invested in hard work pays its dividends in the permanence of the product. And this is the more cause to marvel at the buildings of Pericles, that were made in so little time to last for so long."

It was all done, or almost all, in ten years. The great statue of the Parthenos (Athene) was dedicated at the Great Panathenaia of 438, some of the carvings were still being made. Many of them can now be seen in London, in the British Museum, where they are called the "Elgin Marbles", about which Keats wrote a sonnet. The Greeks are demanding their return to Athens.

In 431 the Peace broke down, and Athens was heading for the disaster of 404. During those years Euripides and Aristophanes wrote most of their surviving plays, Sophocles his last, some of the most beautiful buildings on the Acropolis were completed, Plato was born (428). The writings of the other great historian, Thucydides, make these the best-known years of the history of Athens. Most of Plato's Dialogues are shown as happening then too, for these are the years of Socrates, the culmination of the work of "pre-Socratic" philosophers and sophists.

The first part of the disaster was the plague that ravaged Persia, Egypt and Athens in 430-427, killing a quarter of the population; for some obscure reason, Pericles was blamed! Then his two sons died. In pity, he was re-elected as general, but he died in the autumn of 429 and was irreplaceable.

Thucydides writes his history of this time in a high, solemn style, stressing the terrible disaster that the war between the Greek cities was. In several cases the entire population of captured cities was massacred or sold as slaves. Several times, peace might have been possible, but without Pericles the chance was missed.

By 415 a new leader had appeared in Athens, Alkibiades, whom Socrates tried to educate, and love. He was most handsome and totally vain. He figures in Plato's Symposium. He led a great Athenian army to Sicily on a campaign, then escaped to Sparta when he was called back to Athens, while his army attacked Syracuse. In 413 all the Athenian soldiers were taken prisoner, over 10,000 of them probably, of whom 7,000 were left to die in a "concentration camp" without shelter or real food.

In 411, democracy broke down and an authoritarian oligarchy took power for two years, after which they were so divided that democracy was easily restored. Alkibiades returned to Athens for a time. He was a good leader, but unfortunate, and later he withdrew again. Athens was by now almost completely isolated and although building and drama continued, the loss of life in the fighting also continued. The citizens were deeply divided about the responsibility for the military disasters, the system of justice was breaking down.

In 405 the Spartan leader Lysander captured 170 ships of the Athenian fleet and executed 4,000 Athenian prisoners. All who could took shelter inside the walls of Athens, and after a long siege, when people were dying in the streets, Athens surrendered to Sparta in 404.

Athens, luckily, had such a high reputation for its past deeds against the Persians, that Sparta dared not destroy it. Lysander brought back the oligarchy as a Council of Thirty led by Kritias, which began a reign of terror against the democratic leaders. The "Thirty Tyrants" needed a Spartan bodyguard, but at first there was no organized resistance. Then a small group of seventy Athenian men came back from Thebes and occupied a fortress 10 miles from Athens. They were able to defend it, and soon they were 700. They were able to attack and defeat the main group of Spartans in a surprise attack on their base.

A few days later, 1000 strong now, although with weapons for only 600, they entered Piraeus (the port of Athens on the coast) and when Kritias marched down from Athens with 3,000 men, he was confronted and defeated by this small democratic army, supported by the stone-throwing population of Piraeus which had risen in revolt.

After a few months of confrontation, the democrats entered Athens, the oligarchic leaders were outlawed, and in 403 full democracy was restored in a spirit of forgiving and national harmony. But a new beginning was not so easy. Perhaps the insecurities provoked by so much loss explain why, in 399, the city of Athens condemned to death the 70-year-old Socrates? Yet following him come Plato and Aristotle, the two Greek thinkers whose work remains fundamental even now.

【Philosophy: Socrates】

We only know about Socrates (469 - 399) through Plato's writings, since he himself wrote nothing. The words that Plato gives to Socrates in the early Dialogues, and especially in the *Defense*, may perhaps be a faithful echo of his voice and approach. However, in the later Dialogues it seems clear that Plato is making Socrates say things that Plato himself would wish to say, that Socrates himself would not have said. It is therefore difficult to know just what Socrates himself said and taught. It seems that he was not interested in general systems, and not at all preoccupied with the general question of primal substances.

Rather, we find in Plato a Socrates who has been challenged by the scepticism of the Sophists. He sees that much of what has been taught traditionally may not be true, and that further thought is needed. At the same time, he refuses to accept that all values are relative. His greatest contribution lies perhaps in the way he changes the focus of thought to the definition of certain moral values. For Socrates, philosophy ought to be concerned with helping people to live better lives. The *Defence* shows him enquiring about the exact definition of words such as 'justice,' 'good,' 'truth'. Socrates seems to have thought that virtue was the fruit of knowledge and that when people did wrong, it was because of their ignorance of what was right. His goal in life was to help people think more deeply, so that they could come to a better knowledge of what was good. In that way the city would become a better place.

Socrates' refusal to accept 'ready-made' and badly-thought definitions was to lay the foundation of the discipline of philosophy. His scepticism was systematic, but at the same time he claimed to hear an inner voice (his 'daemon') that told him what was the right thing to do or say. He did not share the fundamental scepticism of the Sophists, who did not recognize any need to look for ultimate answers to ethical questions. Rather he was an idealist not satisfied by anything less than the perfect answers, which he could never find. His fundamental system was to persistently challenge what others said with questions like, "What precisely do you mean by ...?" This method of debate by brief question and answer is known as Socratic *elenchus*.

Almost certainly, Socrates shared earlier thinkers' negative opinion of the ethical standards shown by the gods of Homer, and may have spoken mockingly of them. The religious question was not his main concern, however. Still, his challenging attitude was popular among the young, but must have been deeply offensive to the older generation. He had many enemies, and Aristophanes may have helped turn opinion against him by mocking him in *Clouds*. We see in the *Defense* a man who cannot tolerate unthinking, foolish replies to serious questions, and his tongue must have been biting.

In 399, a charge was made "That Socrates does not believe in the gods in whom the city believes but introduces other and new deities; also, that he corrupts the young." The penalty demanded was death. Plato has given us a text of his *Defense (Apology)* before the citizens' court, and in the *Phaidon* an account of Socrates' last day. Plato was not there, but his account of how Socrates refused to run away, and nobly drank the hemlock (poison), comforting his friends to the end, has given to many a deeper understanding of what "humanism" means.

We probably cannot find anything as powerful until we come to the Gospel stories of the death of Jesus. Socrates was nearly seventy years old, with him the Golden Age of Athens ended.

【Plato】

Plato was born in Athens in 427. His family was aristocratic and he received a fine education in the traditional arts, including poetry and drama, He was already a skilled poet and had composed tragedies which he was intending to submit for the festival competitions when he met Socrates in about 407. He thereupon stopped writing poetry and burned his tragedies, although the radical hostility to the 'imitative' arts he expresses in the *Republic* may have developed only later. He was ill in 399 and was not present at Socrates' last moments. He seems to have been so upset that he left Athens and went travelling, perhaps to meet the Pythagoreans in Italy.

In 389 he visited Syracuse (Sicily) for the first time. There he met the tyrant Dionysios, and his minister Dion. Returning to Athens, Plato bought a small garden outside the walls of Athens, near the shrine of Academos, to be a place where those interested in study and reflection could live a simple life in community, listening to his lectures and discussing together thoughtfully. This marks the beginning of the Academy, the Platonic university which lasted until it was closed by the emperor Justinian in A.D. 529. It taught various doctrines at different periods of its history, dialectical skepticism and Neoplatonic mysticism being the two main ones, but it was always "Plato's Academy." Plato returned to Syracuse later, in the 360s, hoping to educate the son of

Dionysius into the perfect philosopher-king, but that was not possible, and he became part of plots that led to the murder of his friend Dion, as well.

Plato's written works have come down to us complete. They are among the masterpieces of Greek prose. Apart from the poems, and the *Defense (Apology),* they consist of some 25 dialogues, discussions between a number of speakers, usually including Socrates, from which the readers have to go on to think for themselves. Plato did not teach any fixed doctrine, for, he wrote, "Philosophy is not a thing that can be put into words, like other lessons for learning. But from a long communing over the thing itself and from living together, suddenly as though from a flame leaping a gap, a light kindles in the soul; and after that, it finds its own nourishment."

The early Dialogues *(Apology, Laches, Charmides, Crito,* etc) offer portraits of Socrates with his attractive, dynamic character and his ugly body, conversations that pass from the simple to the essential, in the quest for knowledge and virtue, which is the greatest good. The dialogues raise questions about the cssential nature of some vital quality, and end in a failure to find any satisfactory definition.

The great middle period works *(Phaedo, Symposium, Republic,)* are narratives describing an earlier conversation, with vivid details in the descriptions. They culminate in the *Republic,* one of the great works of world culture, with its imaginary 'alternative society' that inspired Mores *Utopia* as well as many other utopian works and satires. The middle period works often discuss the nature of the essential, real and invisible Ideas or Forms (also called "archetypes" or figures), of which the supreme is that of the Good, which is close in some ways to the Christian God.

The later works *(Sophist, Statesman, Timaeus, Laws)* are more obscure. The *Sophist* is about metaphysics, the *Statesman* about government. The *Timaeus* was the only work of Plato's that was translated into Latin and read in the Middle Ages, it discusses the relationship between the visible world and the invisible, body and soul, what in the West came to be seen as Macrocosm (the world of invisible forms) and Microcosm (the visible world reflecting it). The *Laws* return to the nature of government.

【Aristotle】

Aristotle was born in 384; his father was a medical doctor. Aristotle studied at the Academy until Plato's death in 347 but when he was not chosen to succeed Plato as its head, he left and went travelling. He was called to Macedonia to teach the young Alexander he stayed there until about 340. Returning to Athens after Alexander became king, Aristotle founded his own school in a park near the temple of Apollo Lykeios, whence its name : the "Lyceum". He liked to teach small groups while walking together under the trees, so they were called Peripatetics (walkers). After Alexander's death Aristotle fled to Chalkis where he died in 322.

Although he absorbed Plato's teaching deeply, and in his early works taught the doctrines of the immaterial world of Ideas and of the immortality of the soul, Aristotle did not have Plato's love of speculation; rather he was interested in observations of nature. Later he replaced Plato's

Ideas (which are deemed to have independent existence) with the non-transcendent notion of 'concept'. His mind was that of a scientist. Aristotle was interested in encyclopedic knowledge about "things", and in systematizing what could be known about the physical world. The library of collected manuscripts in the Lyceum is the model for all later libraries. There may have been a "Natural History Museum" too. The Lyceum was a research community: Aristotle organized the collection of the Constitutions of 158 Greek states, for example, while other scholars did work on botany, music, physics and the history of science, mathematics, astronomy, theology...

Aristotle's written works have all been lost, although they survived into Roman times. What we have are extensive notes of his lectures. Logic, rhetoric, ethics, political science, physics, metaphysics (presuppositions), biology, were among his courses, and among the most famous of his "works" are the *Analytics*, the *Physics*, the *Metaphysics*, the *Nicomachean Ethics*, the *Politics*, the *Rhetoric*, the *Poetics*. These texts were long hidden after his death, then they were discovered in a cellar in Athens and taken to Rome by Sulla in 84 BC.

Unlike Plato, Aristotle is not interested in the invisible and the speculative. He prefers to list and classify the visible realities, he has a love of categorizing things into neat systems. He invented some of the most important words used in philosophical reflection: "universal and particular", "premise and conclusion", "subject and attribute", "form and matter", "potentiality and actuality". Where Plato's God was the embodiment of a fundamental moral principle, the Good, Aristotle's was an abstract scientific explanation, the First Mover. Aristotle stressed that we can only have certain knowledge of the things we can observe with our senses; he therefore excluded God and the soul from his field of study and seems not to have believed that the human soul had eternal existence.

【Alexander and Hellenism】

Alexander was born in 356. His father was king Philip II of Macedonia, where old-style kingship had continued untouched by distant Athenian models of aristocracy or democracy. When his son was born, Philip was leading his armies in a policy of expansion that soon brought him control of the whole of Greece. Philip was a brilliant leader and strategist and in 338, at the battle of Chaironeia, he defeated the Greeks who had been encouraged to resist him by the great speeches of Demosthenes at Athens. For Philip, Athens was a very special place and he respected its citizens. He had called Aristotle from studies at Plato's Academy to be Alexander's tutor. He also needed its fleet, for he intended to expand his empire into the Middle East, but in 336 Philip was assassinated and Alexander, who had already led the Macedonian cavalry at Chaironea, became king at the age of twenty.

Seeing his age, Thebes rebelled while he was up beyond the Danube. He returned south, captured Thebes in 335, and destroyed it, although he ordered the house where Pindar had lived to be spared. Instead of establishing a firm power base in Greece, Alexander at once set out against the Persians who were in confusion after the murder of their king. He first destroyed their naval bases in Phoenicia, then went to Egypt and founded the city of Alexandria. In 331, he was beyond the

Tigris and after a great victory against the Persians he captured Babylon. In 330 he was in Persepolis, from where he set off northwards. In western Afghanistan he founded the city Alexandria in Arachosia, better known as Kandahar and in 328 he was in the region of Samarkand, and founded "Alexandria at the World's End" (Khojent). By 327, Alexander was master of the whole area now called Iran, and beyond. He was ruling by now, not like a Macedonian king, but like the Persian Great King, before whom all had to bow low.

By 326, Alexander had led his army down into the Punjab (north-west India) but there they refused to go on. They were so far from home and they dreaded fighting the Indian war-elephants. So after exploring the delta of the Indus he turned towards the west. Driven by strange energies, Alexander set out on an expedition to the mouth of the Euphrates through desert and floods, then returned to Babylon and insisted on marrying all his Greek officers to Persian women. He himself had already married Roxana, up in Turkestan, but now he married Statira, a daughter of the last Persian king Darius, as well.

In the summer of 323 he suddenly fell ill and died, without a son yet born, without a successor. The result of his campaigns was a collapse of the Persian Peace, while his settlements were too scattered to be the basis for any permanent new order.

The most significant result of his new cities was the lasting presence of Greek culture in this part of the world so that, when the first king of all India, Asoka, was converted to Buddhism in 259, he turned to the Greek artists still living in India to create a representative art for this new state religion. In this way, many of the artistic forms of Buddhism throughout the Orient derive directly from those developed in Greece.

【After Alexander】

After Alexander's death, the Greeks united in a new anti-Macedonian, Hellenic league but Antipatros, who had been Alexander's governor in Greece, fought back, using soldiers returning from the East, and defeated Athens, destroying its fleet. Democracy was abolished, the great Athenian orator Demosthenes took poison, many emigrated.

The Empire of Alexander broke into three parts, the Macedonian, the Egyptian, and the Asian. Alexander's bodyguard and secretary, Ptolemy ('the warlike') became governor of Egypt, taking back and burying in Alexandria the body of Alexander. He founded there a Hellenistic kingdom that only came to an end in 31 BC, with the deaths of Cleopatra and Mark Antony after the Battle of Actium. He wrote the memoirs of Alexander, using Alexander's own journal, and this became the source for much of what we know.

If Ptolemy planned, his son built; under Ptolemy II were built in Alexandria the Pharos (lighthouse), the Museum (Temple of the Muses) and the Library designed to contain everything important ever written in Greek. He also built a canal linking the Nile to the Red Sea. The rulers of Alexandria celebrated the cult of the deified Alexander. Alexandria became the main intellectual center of the Hellenistic Age it was entirely Macedonian in its ruling class, governing the native Egyptians firmly with well-organized bureaucracy.

The commander of Alexander's foot-soldiers, Seleukos, gained the Asian possessions and would have taken Macedonia too, but a son of Ptolemy who was his friend murdered him in 280. His son was called Antiochus, which became the dynastic name and was given to a number of cities of the "Seleucid" empire centered in modern Syria. The history of Palestine (Judea) at this time is that of the power struggle between the Seleucids and the Ptolemies, these latter keeping control until 198, when Antiochus III incorporated it into his Seleucid empire.

Macedonia, having lost its royal line, became weaker, although it kept control of the Greek cities until 229 when Athens sold the official copies of Aeschylus, Sophocles and Euripides to Ptolemy III and bought her freedom, proclaiming herself a neutral city, friendly to all powers. This enabled Athens to become the City of Philosophers, the University city.

【The Hellenistic Age】

Athens was still the philosophical centre of the Greek-speaking world, but Alexandria also attracted many scholars and they were encouraged by the endowments of the Ptolemies. Euclid systematized geometry c. 300 BC in his "Elements" while teaching there.

Around 280-265, Aristarchos of Samos evolved the theory that the sun is at the centre of the universe, with the earth and other planets revolving around it, and he tried to measure the distances of sun and moon from the earth, but failed. The Athenian Stoics were shocked because they thought of the stars as divine powers. Because he taught that the planets revolved in perfect circles the theory of Aristarchos did not correspond to actual observation and was rejected in favor of that formulated later (in the 2nd century A.D.) by the Alexandrian astronomer Ptolemy. The Ptolemaic model of the universe, in which the earth is the fixed center around which the sun and stars turn, continued to be accepted until the 16th century when the Polish astronomer Copernicus returned to the theory of Aristarchos, corrected it by giving the planets elliptical orbits, and provoked the 'Copernican Revolution'.

Eratosthenes, the librarian at Alexandria after 250, calculated the circumference of the earth by comparing the shadows cast at Assuan and Alexandria on midsummer's day. He was only 10 per cent wrong. Other scholars, mathematicians and historians, developed an ever more encyclopedic system of learning. Eratosthenes was the first scholar to call himself a "philologist" (lover of learning). The great library of Alexandria prepared lists of the authors of the various genres whose works they either had or wished to obtain, and this 'Canon' marks the beginnings of literary history and criticism.

Rome and the Roman Empire

The story of the founding of Rome by the twins Romulus and Remus is a strange Founding Myth. According to its account, Remus mocked Romulus' work by jumping over the scarcely-begun walls; Romulus then killed his brother and founded Rome alone, giving it his own name. Fratricidal rivalry is not usually considered to be a good beginning for an enterprise. The twins, said to have been suckled by a wolf as babies, were later described as descendants of Aeneas from Troy. That reflects a desire to connect Rome with the splendors of ancient Greek tradition and mythology.

The traditional date for the founding of Rome was 753 B.C. Archeology shows that by 575, if not earlier, small villages on the site of Rome were beginning to coalesce into a larger city-state (in Latin urbs,) with advances in civilized living being made under Etruscan influence. The first temple, of Jupiter on the Capitol, was built at this time. The Etruscans, whose still-undeciphered language was not of Indo-European origin, lived in areas near Rome and their artistic culture has left some remarkable clay statues of adult couples. They were finally completely assimilated into the expanding Roman culture.

【Early Roman History】

In 510, the last Roman king, Tarquin the Proud, was driven out of Rome and an aristocratic republic established, with the imperium (supreme power) vested in two magistrates, later called consuls, elected each year.

The kings had naturally had a Council and this developed into the Senate, which was the main governing body of Rome, composed of men who had held public office, so similar to the Athenian Boule. The Senate served as the symbol and voice of the State, even when its power was reduced under the emperors. In times of crisis a dictator (similar to a Greek tyrant) might be appointed by the Senate to lead the people.

The citizens of Rome were divided into two classes, the aristocratic patrician families and the mass of the plebs, and much of the constitution of Rome arose in the struggle for power, as the lower class plebs established their right to representation, such as tribunes, and an Assembly. In the end, compromise led to solutions which, in Greece, were never found, partly perhaps because the expansion of Roman power over the Italian peninsula always gave the lower classes chances of becoming rich. The city soon developed a system of food subsidies, by which each citizen was entitled to free bread, as a means of reducing social tensions.

Greek attempts to assert power obliged Rome to exercise its military power across Italy and by the end of wars against the Greek Pyrrhus in 275, Rome had taken control of the whole Italian mainland. Pyrrhus gained two "Pyrrhic victories" against Rome between 280 and 278. (A "Pyrrhic victory" is one in which, although you win a battle, you lose the war). The Romanizing of Italy was done slowly, by colonizing, by treaty and by influence, until most people were speaking Latin, using Roman laws, and seeing the advantage of being Roman citizens. In 273, Ptolemaic Egypt recognized the importance of Rome. The expansion of Roman control over the Greek settlements in Southern Italy and Sicily by 241, brought Greek culture fully into Roman life. The Romans organized, first Sicily, then other overseas territories, as provinces, the units of government that were to compose the Empire.

The First Punic War was fought in Sicily against the power of Carthage, Rome's main rival (the word Punic is the same as Phoenician, for Carthage was a Phoenician colony). It ended in Roman triumph, Carthage being forced to leave Sicily. Then Rome drove the Carthaginians out of the western islands of Sardinia and Corsica too. Between 237 and 219, the Carthaginian generals Hamilcar, Hasdrubal and Hannibal took control of Spain and in 218 Hannibal launched an attack on Northern Italy. His exploit in marching an army of 30,000 men over the Alps in winter provoked the admiration of the Romans.

The Romans sent an army to Spain to prevent reinforcements arriving. They drove the Carthaginians out of Spain and thus isolated Hannibal while avoiding direct battle. They then invaded Africa and at last Hannibal was recalled to defend Carthage itself in 203. He had spent 16 years in Italy and left undefeated. He died by his own hand in 183 while Carthage was finally destroyed in 146, after a third Punic war; but Rome had already ensured in the Second Punic War its international superiority for centuries.

After the destruction of Carthage, Rome took control of the fertile lands of North Africa, then slowly expanded control north of the Alps and towards what is now Yugoslavia. In about 120, the southern area of Gaul (now called France) was formed into a province (it is still known as Provence). After serving for 20 years, each Roman soldier was entitled to a grant of farming land to which he could retire. Such provinces provided the land needed. Meanwhile, the Romans had been drawn into Greece, where they sacked Corinth in 146 and transported vast masses of Greek art to Rome, where Greek philosophers were already lecturing by 155, although there was never a true university in Rome.

【Civil War】

With the wealth of Greece and Carthage, Rome became immensely rich, and this led to increasing corruption across the empire, which in turn led to widespread resentment of the "greedy Italians." The structures of administration had still to be created. In Italy, unrest came mainly from the slaves and the rural poor (uprisings in 135, 103). Germanic tribes, too, were already invading Italy and had to be pushed back (102). The discontent built up into civil war, which could only be won by concessions. By about 90 B.C., all Italians were automatically Roman citizens, but all of this had made the Army, especially the Commander, immensely powerful. For many years, the Commander, and consul was Marius. But in 88 Sulla marched on Rome, opposing Marius, and the period of Civil War began, the Republic having already lost much of its credibility. In 83 Sulla set himself up as dictator, in place of Cinna, but soon they both had to retire.

In 70, the general Pompey was consul with Crassus, and these two military leaders imposed their rule against that of the Senate. In 67 Pompey became Tribune, war-leader, and established the Province of Syria in 64. At the same time Julius Caesar (born in 100 B.C.) was rising in power at Rome. In 63, the consul Cicero unmasked a revolutionary conspiracy by a group led by Cataline, but by now Crassus and Julius Caesar were plotting to share power while Pompey had retired into private life. Since the Senate would not accept their demands, the result was a coalition uniting Crassus, Pompey and Caesar, called the First Triumvirate (60). Caesar, chosen as consul in 59, left to capture the northern parts of Gaul in a long campaign (58-50) which he described in his great book "The Gallic War" (Caesar is one of the greatest prose writers of ancient times). Gaul (now France) became part of the Empire, stretching from the English Channel to the Rhine. Caesar even crossed into Britain in 55 and 54, but did not establish any lasting control.

It was Julius Caesar who finally established the modern (solar) calendar with 365 days (or 366 in leap years) and twelve months. The Romans called the first day of the month the Kalends, the 5th or 7th the Nones, and the 13th or 15th the Ides (the later date for the 31-day months) and calculated dates by counting back from those, which had their origin in the older lunar calendar. The year began on March 1st, and this was only changed in the 18th century, which explains why the names of the months September - December do not now correspond to their position in the calendar (Sept = 7, Oct = 8, Nov = 9, Dec = 10). Roman years were often numbered by counting from 753 (the foundation of the city, in Latin Ab urbe condita, AUC)

Crassus having died in 53, the conflict between Caesar and Pompey became open war. Julius Caesar crossed the Rubicon, entering Italy without the Senate's permission, which signified civil war, and then defeated Pompey's armies in Spain (49) and Greece (48). He followed Pompey to Egypt, where he spent the winter fighting Ptolemy XIII, and having an affair with Cleopatra, whom he installed as Queen of Egypt and who bore his only son. He then returned to Asia Minor, for a victory at Zela (47), where he said the famous veni, vidi, vici (I came, I saw, I conquered). In Africa (46) and Spain again (45), he won other battles, each victory weakening the Republican cause. Caesar, as dictator, was clearly a personal ruler, whether or not he intended to change the basic constitution and become king. In 44, after he had been made Dictator for life, he received almost all the royal honors At last, a group of conspirators under Cassius and Brutus assassinated Caesar in the Senate House on the Ides of March (March 15) 44 B.C.. He fell at the foot of Pompey's statue.

【Augustus and the Roman Empire】

Julius Caesar had no legal son to be his heir, so he named the son of his niece, Caius Octavius (63BC - A.D. 14), to be his heir. In 43, after Caesar's death, Octavius was recognized as Caesar's "son" with the name Octavianus, and in the same year he, Mark Antony and Lepidus, were named Triumvirs. In 42 they defeated the Republicans under Brutus and Cassius, both of whom killed themselves. In 42, also, Julius Caesar was named a "god" and thus Octavian became "son of god." In 41, Antony was in Egypt, where he met Cleopatra, with whom he too began an affair, although he made a political marriage with Octavian's sister Octavia in 40.

In 36, Lepidus fell and, while Antony was busy in the East, Octavian took power over Italy and the West. In 31, at the naval Battle of Actium, Antony and Cleopatra were defeated. They killed themselves and Octavian became supreme ruler, the Empire was at peace. This Augustan Peace which lasted throughout his reign was marked by the construction of the Ara Pacis in Rome, and the Augustan Age was later felt to have been a Golden Age. In 29, the Senate confirmed the title of Imperator (Emperor) which Octavian had been using since 38. His power was based on his prestige, but he tried to make the Empire aware of the values of Roman tradition by encouraging writers to express the imperial vision. Among them were Virgil and Horace.

In 27 he received the title Augustus, "supreme," indicating his *de facto* position, and the month August got its name at this time. He had become a "constitutional emperor," ruling with the support of the Senate and Roman People (Senatus Populus que Romanus SPQR was the symbol carried at the head of the armies), but as he was more and more honored as a god, his position was quite unique. Under his rule, the provinces became truly an Empire.

We might note that in A.D. 6, Judea (the area around Jerusalem) became a minor Province by annexation, after the deposition of Archelaus who had succeeded Herod the Great (died 4 B.C.). It was to be ruled by Procurators, nominated for 10 years. In 27, Pontius Pilate became Procurator. Galilee was not part of Roman Judaea, it was ruled as a Tetrarchy by Herod Antipas, under whose rule Jesus of Nazareth lived, and by whose command John the Baptist was executed.

【Early Roman Literature】

Rome has nothing to compare with Homer and Hesiod, Plato and Aristotle. It developed no great literary or philosophical tradition. There are the plays written by Terence and Plautus from the period 200-150, but otherwise nothing of note from before the time of Caesar and Augustus. At the time of Caesar, the leading Roman statesman was Cicero (born 106) whose full name was Marcus Tullius Cicero, so that he was also known (in Shakespeare etc.) as "Tully". He was opposed to Antony after the assassination of Caesar and he was murdered by Antony's agents in 43 B.C.. He had studied at the Academy in Athens, where he learned to present mostly Stoic morality in a simple, undogmatic way.

His main works are his Orations (speeches made in the course of his career as a lawyer and political figure), his 931 letters to 99 different people, and writings on rhetoric and style. As a philosophical figure, he wrote on political theory (De Republica, a dialogue), on ethical and on theological questions. He was deeply influenced by the Stoics but adopted an independent line on some questions. His main doctrine is that of humanitas, the qualities of mind and character that make a man civilized. A true Man should respect all men because humanity is worthy of respect. (The Stoics taught the universal Brotherhood of Man, based on the notion that each individual contains a spark of the same divine fire). No law, he said, can make a wrong thing right or a right thing wrong. The moral thought of Cicero has deeply marked the thinkers of Europe: Luther, Montaigne, Locke, Hume. He was mainly familiar as a moral thinker in the Middle Ages, but at the Renaissance his influence as a stylist in prose, as the model of Latin style, was enormous.

Lucretius (94-55) is known only for his great philosophical poem *De Rerum Natura*, a didactic poem in six books exposing the theories of Epicurus in order to free people's minds from superstitious fear of gods, or trust in Fortune. All things, he says, are the result of the random motions of an infinite number of atoms moving in infinite space. There is therefore no immortality of the soul, so that it is foolish to fear death. This is a poem full of artistry, one of the great intellectual poems.

Sallust (86-35) was one of the first Roman historians, writing about the period of Marius and the first stages of the decline of the Republic.

Julius Caesar himself wrote "Commentaries" on his wars, seven books on the campaign in Gaul, three more on the Civil War, describing each stage in clear, simple prose. These have been much studied, for Caesar was one of the greatest generals ever, a master-strategist.

【Augustan Literature】

The Augustan Age was later often seen as a Golden Age, because of the quality of the writers, because it was a age of peace, because Rome was rebuilt in imperial style. Yet it was also an age of failure and disappointment, because Augustus was an authoritarian dictator, an autocrat who swept away the last democratic forms of the Republic and took control of every sector of life. Augustus established the Empire as it was to survive for 400 years, with a broadly unified culture that would spread across Western Europe, bringing many of the best things that had first been discovered by Greece. Augustus wished to give his people a higher vision of morality, of human dignity, and used art for that purpose.

Virgil (70-19) was born near Mantua, studied at Cremona, Milan, Rome. He was deeply influenced by the poems of Catullus and by the perfections of rhythms and form practiced by the Alexandrians. At the time of Caesar's death he went to live in the countryside near Naples, and here he began his bucolic (pastoral) *Eclogues*. These caught the attention of Octavian's rich and powerful advisor, Maecenas, the model rich patron of literature, who brought Virgil into the service of the rising future Augustus. The *Eclogues* were followed soon by the *Georgics*, written after he had met Horace. Later he began to write the *Aeneid* for Augustus. He went to finish it and study in Athens, from which he returned with Augustus in 19, but fell ill and died on the way home.

The *Eclogues* are modeled on the *Idylls* of Theocritus, but blend the Greek and the Italian landscapes. The action is located in Arcadia, an idealized land of shepherds acting as a symbolic contrast to the corruptions of the contemporary city, so that "pastoral" poetry is satiric as well as escapist. The delicate sentiments and the pure music of Virgil's *Eclogues* have inspired many later poets, including Sidney and Spenser.

The *Georgics* are presented as a guide to being a good farmer, but the quality of the poetry shows that this is no mere handbook. These poems underlie many others written later about the details of ordinary daily life, especially working life, and the pleasures of rural activity. But they also show that there is a religious mystery revealed by contact with nature. For Dryden these were "the best poems of the best poet."

The *Aeneid* relates the story of Aeneas in 12 books. An epic of the legendary origins of Rome, with a strong unity of action, inspired by Homer. The style is highly polished, artificial, quite unlike the popular style of Homer. During the Middle Ages, it was read as an allegory of the human life but from Petrarch on, it was also seen as a model to be imitated by Renaissance writers of epic.

For Western culture, no work is more influential than the *Aeneid.* Homer was unknown for centuries, the Middle Ages knew only his name and had no Latin translation of his epics, in fact he was taken for a liar because there existed better-known Latin prose stories of the same events told from the Trojan point of view. These stories, bearing the names of Dares Phrygius ("The Fall of Troy") and Dictys of Crete ("Diary of the Trojan War"), were the main source of stories about Troy until the mid-17th century.

The *Aeneid* is equally a continuation of the Trojan side, Aeneas being shown as the son of Venus and a Trojan father, Anchises, in the Iliad, where he is second to Hector. The *Aeneid* is written with intense artistry, with all Virgil's sensitivity and compassion. It shows the foundation of Rome being prepared through great suffering, near-despair, and human weakness, thanks to a scheme of divine providence.

Since printing began in Western Europe, the *Aeneid* has been published in at least one new edition every year; from Roman times until then it had been read continuously, even when no other classical poetry was esteemed. Virgil was considered to have been a Prophet of Christ, and was given religious respect. He is a basic influence for Dante, Shakespeare, Milton, Pope, Victor Hugo, Tennyson...

【The Aeneid】 (Summary)

In Book 1 the Trojan survivors, led by Aeneas, escape a terrible storm and arrive in North Africa. There they are brought by Venus to the court of Dido, Queen of Carthage, who falls in love with Aeneas. She asks to hear his story, which occupies Books 2 and 3, with the destruction of Troy and his travels. They have settled down into a quiet life together, but without any wedding ceremony. In Book 4 Mercury is sent with a message from the gods, urging Aeneas to remember his mission to go to Italy and found a new Troy there. His departure causes Dido to commit suicide and is given as the reason for the centuries of war between Carthage and Rome in the future.

Arriving back in Sicily, Aeneas the "True" organizes Games to commemorate the first anniversary of his father's death there, before the journey to Carthage (Book 5). From there they sail up to Cumae, near Naples, and visit the Sibyl (oracle of Apollo) in her cave. After an oracle on their future plans, Aeneas asks permission to go down into the Underworld and meet his father's spirit. He is given instructions and makes the journey (Book 6), one of the most famous parts of the

Aeneid.

Once at the Tiber, difficulties and fighting return (Book 7), but the spirit of Tiber encourages Aeneas to enter Latium. He sails up to the site of future Rome, where Arcadians are living, and visits the Capitol and the Forum, still just rocks and fields. For future battle, Venus obtains Armour from Vulcan, with a shield picturing the future story of Rome (Book 8). The remaining books (Books 9-12) describe the great battles and struggle between Aeneas and Turnus for control of the land, with Aeneas' last gesture of killing Turnus an unnecessary act of revenge for the death of Pallas, when Turnus was already beaten. The poem was left incomplete at Virgil's death.

The morality of the *Aeneid* is "Avoid excess, be true." Its basic theme is the importance of harmony and reconciliation, true nobility in living.

Horace (65-8) was born in a simple family, went to study at the University of Athens, then served under Brutus, but survived the defeat at Philippi (42) and was introduced to Maecenas by Virgil and entered the service of Octavian, who enjoyed his company. His combination of great poetic skill with a basically humorous attitude to life made him the great model for English writers such as Pope.

The *Epodes* are the earlier works, iambic poems in which Horace adopts a tone of bitterness, ferocity, which is often found not to be "real"; they are about love problems, politics, or are humorous exercises.

They show refined techniques in epigram etc., derived from the Hellenistic Greek poetry.

The *Satires* follow a genre invented by Lucilius (died 101), the personal, autobiographical satire, about opinions, adventures, food, family, friends, morality, but Horace is much less bitter, far more humorous; a stream of anecdotes interrupts the flow of ideas, and we never know when Horace is being ironic because he mocks himself as much as everyone else. He uses a form of the epic hexameter, passing from the high style to the very relaxed, and this link between epic and satire is recalled in the 17-18th century English "mock-epic."

The *Odes* (*Carmina*) are designed to display Horace's great technical skill, modeled on the Greek poets, both Sappho and the Alexandrians. They are not "pure" lyrics, but explore many forms and situations, often expressing directly political comments, which until this were only found in epic forms of poetry. For Petrarch as for Ben Jonson, these were a major model, and they inspired Marvell's "Horatian Ode."

The *Epistles*(letters) are his own inventions, written after the Odes (from 20 B.C.), verse letters in which it is possible to deal with any subject in a personal, conversational way: how to get on with great men, the dangers of avarice, the value of the simple life, town versus country etc. They are not "real" letters, addressed to a particular person, but exercises in style. They were very influential from the Renaissance period onwards, from Donne to Pope especially.

Ars Poetica(Art of Poetry) is also a verse epistle, skillful and humorous, but although it talks about epic and drama, it is not quite clear what message it contains.

Livy (64-A.D. 12?) is the great historian of Rome. He wrote a history from the beginnings, in 142 books, of which only 35 have survived. He exposes the history of Rome in vivid prose, full of descriptions, that make it a "prose epic," a form of literature. It is given a basic moral structure (Livy came from a very strict family in Padua) by the idea of old Rome as a place of discipline, simplicity, piety, virtue, all values lost in later corruption by luxury and avarice.

Propertius (54-16), the most "artistic" of the Latin poets, elaborate, witty and energetic like John Donne, is difficult. He gave the name "Cynthia" to his lady, who seems to be real.

Ovid (43-A.D. 17) became famous as a poet in the generation after the death of Virgil and Horace, by 8 A.D. he was the most famous poet in Rome, but then he displeased Augustus (How? We have no clear information) and he was exiled to Tomis on the Black Sea, a dangerous place on the edge of the Empire, where he died.

Ovid wrote all his works except the Metamorphoses in elegiac couplets. The Amores, a collection of love poems, suggesting a final rejection of love-conventions, translated by Marlowe, influenced Donne. The *Heroides* (Epistles from Heroic Women) are mostly verse epistles or dramatic monologues written/spoken by famous women to absent husbands or lovers; a second group has pairs of letters in which the man writes/speaks first. These are explorations of the psychology of passion, of what we call "romantic love," the oppositions between the sexes exist in unresolved tension.

The *Ars Amatoria*(Art of Loving) is a parody of normal didactic poetry, teaching the arts of seduction and intrigue to men (books 1 & 2) and women (book 3). It must have shocked, but Ovid's "apology" or retraction, the Remedia Amoris (the Cure for Love), is no more serious. In the Middle Ages, Ovid's psychology of Love was immensely popular, especially in France, where it underlies what is often known as "courtly love."

The *Metamorphoses*(Transformations), an epic poem in 15 books in epic hexameters, show the transformations found in old legends, from the beginnings of time until Julius Caesar. Ovid wished to be made immortal by this work, which is inspired by Alexandrian poetry. It is essentially a collection of fragmentary stories, anecdotes united by an overall thematic framework and by Ovid's narrative skill. The more philosophical theme of "mutability and permanence" stands to affirm a basically optimistic outlook. These stories are the main source of medieval and Renaissance knowledge of Greek mythology, interpreted in the Middle Ages in a moralizing, allegorical way. The Metamorphoses was often read and translated in England, especially by Caxton (1480) and by Arthur Golding (1567-7) whose translation had a great influence on Elizabethan poetry, including Shakespeare, who probably also read the original Latin.

Ovid, with Virgil, is one the first "literary poets," his poems show how much he had read of other poets. But he is writing about human emotions, exploring the heart and its passions. He has enormous technical skills over language and meter, but above all a marvelous imagination, which may be serious or amused. In any case, he teaches us to be more human at every point. Compared with the other Augustans, he is a man of freedom and sensitivity, aware of the good that exists in life. He and Virgil are the two poets who were read continuously, who were as familiar in the 12th century as in the 16th.

【The Emperors after Augustus】

"I found Rome brick, I left it marble" said Augustus. The Rome of the empire, of which we see the remains still, was begun under Augustus. But he had no son or grandson to succeed him. Tiberias, a brilliant general, was chosen and adopted, and became Emperor when Augustus died in 14 A.D.. In his reign there was already a feeling of insecurity, there were mutinies in the provinces. Tiberias withdrew to the island of Capri in 26 and never returned to Rome. He died there, insane, in 37, in a climate of terror. Under his rule Pontius Pilate had Jesus executed in Jerusalem.

He was followed by Gaius whose universally-known name is Caligula (little boot). He is the first of the monster-emperors, of immense cruelty, probably insane, accepting honors which made him equal to a god in his lifetime, stirring up revolt among the Jews by a plan to put a statue of himself in the temple at Jerusalem. He was assassinated in 41, to be followed by the more reasonable Claudius. He was handicapped and physically weak, and became emperor by chance when the soldiers who had killed Caligula found him hiding in the Palace. He was interested in administration. In his days, in 43, Britain became a province of the Roman Empire and the city of London was founded on the Thames at the lowest place where a crossing could be made; London was to become the largest Roman city north of the Alps.

Claudius had at least four wives, the last of whom was his niece, Agrippina, who had already a son, Nero, whom Claudius adopted in 50 as guardian to his own son Britannicus. Agrippina, at first very powerful, but later rejected by Nero, turned to Britannicus, who should have become Emperor, as Claudius' son. In 54 Claudius died, perhaps thanks to some mushrooms given him by Agrippina, and Nero became Emperor. Britannicus had lost his right to the throne, and was poisoned, probably on Nero's orders, in 55. Nero was interested in poetry and art, thanks to his tutor Seneca who became his main advisor for a time.

In 59, encouraged by his mistress Poppaea, the wife of his friend Otho (who was to be emperor for 2 months in 69), Nero arranged the murder of his mother, who had perhaps been plotting his death. In 62 Seneca retired from imperial service, leaving Nero completely out of control. He then divorced and murdered his wife, Octavia, in order to marry Poppaea (whom Otho had wisely divorced, he himself going to live in Spain). In 65 Poppaea died of a kick Nero gave her.

Nero was fond of Greek styles in art, and of gymnastics. He built a Gymnasium and founded Games for young men (Juvenalia) in Rome. He also wrote poetry which was loudly acclaimed. He was highly unpopular at Rome. In 64 a fire destroyed one half of the city; there is a report that he caused it ("Nero fiddled while Rome burned"), at least he took over a lot of the land thus cleared to build a vast palace, and decided quite arbitrarily to blame the Christians of Rome for the blaze, slaughtering many. According to widely accepted legend the martyrs included the apostles Peter and Paul (cf. the film Quo Vadis). Peter is said to have been crucified while Paul was beheaded.

In 65, a plot to assassinate Nero was betrayed and many were executed or forced to commit suicide, including the great Stoic and writer of tragedies, Seneca, and the epic poet Lucan. By 66 the Jews were in revolt, Nero sent Vespasian to pacify them and left for Greece. By now Nero could not tolerate any rivalry, and forced generals to commit suicide because they were successful! In Greece he won the top prize in all the Games and Festivals, while there was a famine in Rome. Executions continued. Revolts broke out in Gaul, Spain, Africa. At last Nero fled from Rome and committed suicide in June 68.

【Literary Figures of the Post-Augustan Period】

Phaedrus (15 B.C.-50) ought to be known for his adaptations into Latin of Aesop's *Fables* since his work established the fable, especially the beast fable, as a serious genre.

Seneca (4 B.C.-65) was above all a philosopher, Stoic and moralizing, but many of his works are lost. He is notable in literary history because his Latin versions of nine tragedies (*Hercules Furens, Medea, Troades, Phaedra, Agamemnon, Oedipus, Hercules Oetaeus, Phoenissae, Thyestes*) showed the Renaissance a form of classical tragedy that it found more congenial than the austere Greek originals. Seneca's tragedies are designed to be read in 'closet performance', not acted in a theater They are static, and in high style. The presence of ghosts, tyrants, madmen, nurses, traitors, of high emotions expressed in elaborate rhetoric, of violent events, and other such elements in Renaissance tragedy are all signs of Senecan influence. His work is designed to illustrate the Stoic idea that passion is essentially destructive; passion and revenge unleash the hounds of hell, and the innocent suffer as much as the guilty, while the gods remain above, indifferent.

Seneca's prose works are marked by noble humanism and moral enlightenment. His style is epigrammatic, curt, and influenced the change in English prose style in about 1600. Until then, Cicero had been the model. Erasmus edited him, Montaigne chose him and Plutarch as his favorite writers. The English Essays of Francis Bacon show strong Senecan influence in their use of philosophical epigrams.

Petronius, too, committed suicide in 65 after loosing Nero's favor. He is the author of one work, the Satyricon, which many consider the first novel. It is a kind of Menippean Satire, combining lyric and mock epic, poetry with prose. It is full of low-class and disreputable heroes, humor of situation and lively, realistic dialogue that reminds one of Charles Dickens. Its structure is episodic, like the picaresque novel.

【The Later Empire】

Astonishingly, the Empire survived the excesses of Nero; the administration laid down by Augustus and Claudius did its job, even in the confusion that followed them. At first, after Nero's death, the Praetorian Guard (in charge of imperial security at Rome) and the Senate, chose Galba from Spain as emperor. The next year the Guard acclaimed Otho and killed Galba. The armies along the Rhine chose Vitellius, there was a battle which Otho lost, he committed suicide. In the East, the armies had chosen Vespasian; they marched on Rome, there was fierce fighting and Vitellius was killed. Vespasian ruled as Emperor for 10 years.

The long Jewish Revolt, centered in Jerusalem, was finally crushed by a Roman army led by Vespasian's son Titus who in 70 captured Jerusalem, destroying the city and the Temple, removing the veil and sacred ornaments to Rome. This event was recorded on the Arch of Titus that still stands near the Colosseum in Rome. From this moment, the Jewish identity could only continue in Diaspora (dispersion). In fact, since the deportation by Nebuchadnezzar in 587, there had been large communities of Jews living in Babylon; they remained there until the 20th century when most if not all went to live in Israel. In Alexandria one third of the population was Jewish at the time of Claudius.

The destruction of the Temple did not mean the end of Judaism, which continued with the local Synagogue as the center of worship, with community rituals marking each stage of life, and with the annual festivals including the family-centered Passover Meal with its final "Next year in Jerusalem!" Finally, in 135, exasperated by continuing Jewish revolts, Hadrian built a Graeco-Roman city on top of the ruins of Jerusalem and forbade Jews to live in it.

Under Vespasian, the Empire knew peace and ordered government, which could be continued because he left two sons who followed him as emperor, Titus (emperor 79-81) and Domitian (emperor 81-96). The role of the emperor now became clearer; he was effectively a monarch with absolute powers. Under Vespasian and Titus, this was expressed in good government, but Domitian, Titus' younger brother, after a good beginning began a reign of terror from 93, in which philosophers were banished from Italy and many people were executed. The emperor saw plots everywhere but at last his wife and others succeeded in murdering him in 96.

The new emperor is counted as the first of the "Five Good Emperors": Nerva (only ruled for 2 years), Trajan (98-117), Hadrian (117-138), Antoninus (138-161), Marcus Aurelius (161-180). One important factor was that all these men chose their successor as "the best man available," having no sons of their own. As soon as Marcus Aurelius made his son his successor, corruption returned. In this time, the Roman presence in Britain was being confirmed, and Hadrian is still remembered for Hadrian's Wall (built 122-7), which divides England from the lands to the north, stretching originally from coast to coast at the level of modern Newcastle-upon-Tyne. The fierce Pictish tribes of the North were too strong for the legions.

This is the great age of the Roman cities across the Empire. Peace meant that economic development became possible, the great road system was expanded, trade went beyond the frontiers, to Scandinavia and China. This is the age that built the Colosseum, Trajan's Forum, the Pantheon in Rome, while theaters, baths, aqueducts, schools and libraries spread across Europe, the Middle East, and North Africa. This is the Silver Age of Latin Literature. At the same time, the Empire was becoming more international, more Oriental too, and Christianity was not the only

Eastern religion spreading at this time, but it was to outlive all the rest.

【The Writers of the Silver Age】

Quintillian (30-100?) is only known by one work, "On the Training of an Orator," in which he outlines a traditional system of education based on speech-making. In the Renaissance, many scholars were tutors to high-class children and his ideas appealed to Erasmus, Vives etc. At the end, he gives a picture of the finished product, a Roman gentleman perfect in morals and diction. Pope refers to his suggestions about good reading in the Essay on Criticism.

Statius (40-96) left only one work that has survived, the epic *Thebaid* which was highly esteemed in the Middle Ages by Dante and Chaucer. It tells of the fratricidal conflict between Eteocles and Polynices for control of Thebes, ending in their deaths (they kill each other). Creon refuses burial to Polynices but Antigone and his wife perform the rites. Theseus of Athens intervenes, kills Creon, and destroys Thebes. The work is no longer admired.

Martial (40-104) has left us fifteen books with more than 1500 epigrams, often a single couplet. Some have a "sting" that is closer to satire than the Greek epigrams had ever been. But the humor ("wit") goes with deep understanding of humanity. Martial's epigrams were essential for the art of 17th-century poetry: Ben Jonson, John Donne, Herrick, Cowley. Renaissance critics distinguished between different tones of epigram: honeyed, pungent, mordant, ridiculous and foul.

Pliny the Younger (61-114) is best known for his 10 books of letters, 247 letters to 105 people. They were prepared for publication, so are more artificial than those of Cicero, but it is Pliny who taught the West the art of literary letters, a form of essay. One of the most famous letters contains his description of the eruption of Vesuvius in 79 which destroyed Pompeii, in which his uncle died. Equally important is his letter to the Emperor Trajan, in which he asks how he should deal with the Christians in the province of Asia Minor he had been sent to govern.

Juvenal (50-127) is the greatest of the ancient satirists, fierce where Horace was amused, considering the evils of his age with "harsh, wild laughter." Some of the topics of his poems are: hypocritical philosophers, the difficulties of being poor, the faults of women, the evils of pride and ambition, the cruelties of people. He was popular in the Middle Ages and the Renaissance. Donne and other young men of his time enjoyed his caustic approach. Dryden was the first to translate him while adapting his references to contemporary situations, Boileau in France, Pope and Dr. Johnson, Burke, Hugo, Flaubert, Byron, all drew on his 16 surviving poems. His vision of the world is always on the darker side, his struggle is to remain human despite all the wickedness he sees.

Tacitus (55-117?) is a chronicler, a historian. He tells us almost all we know about the events between the death of Augustus and the death of Nero in his Annals, and is the source for Robert Graves' novels about Claudius, for the film "Quo Vadis," as well as for Racine's Britannicus, Ben Jonson's Sejanus (in which Shakespeare acted) etc. He is also a vital source of knowledge about the Germanic tribes in his Germania; some of them were later to cross the Channel and become the Anglo-Saxons while others took control of Italy. He even describes Britain in his Agricola.

Suetonius (69-140) is the founder of modern biography, in his lost De Viris Illustribus, in his "Lives of the Poets" and his "Lives of the Twelve Caesars." After him, history came to be seen in a biographical perspective, and thus he inspired St. Jerome's De Viris Illustribus (392), Einhard's Life of Charlemagne (820), William of Malmesbury's History of the English Kings (1127) and all that follow. His lives are told without prejudice or rhetoric, facts speak for themselves, and since the people he describes were so fascinating, his lives are reported like "case-histories."

At the same time, but living in Greece and writing in Greek, lived Plutarch (50-120). For the last thirty years of his fife he was priest at Delphi and wished to revive the ancient Greek spirit. He is most famous for his Lives, although he wrote very many other works, mostly philosophical as with his Moralia. His Lives contain biographical portraits of 50 great men, some legendary like Theseus and Romulus, some almost contemporary like Julius Caesar and Brutus. Mostly they are written in pairs, with moralizing comparisons attached. The stories he tells are vivid, the narrative memorable, the style varied. Many of the Lives follow a pattern of family background - education - youth - climax - change of fortune, which helped to inspire the Renaissance historical tragedy. In France, he was translated by Amyot in 1559, this was then put into English by Sir Thomas North (1579), giving Shakespeare his material for Julius Caesar and other plays. Montaigne, Dryden, Rousseau and the French Revolutionaries all drew on him. In Plutarch's Lives, history is seen becoming literature.

Marcus Aurelius is unique among the emperors in being also famous as a writer. He was much engaged in provincial wars, in Syria and Egypt, etc. During his spare time he made notes on thoughts which struck him. Because of his own personality, and the difficulties surrounding him, these have great intensity, although the Stoic ideas expressed in these Meditations are not very new. It is a work which has appealed to thoughtful men of action over the centuries.

【The Decline and Fall】

After 200, civil war and chaos returned, although for most people normal life continued. The slaves remained slaves, the poor remained poor. Many emperors came and went, now from many countries, as they were imposed by military coups in different areas. Germanic tribes were pressing on the Eastern frontiers, and there were many problems. At last Diocletian (emperor 284-305) decided to divide the Empire into two parts, Greek-speaking to the East, Latin-speaking to the West, establishing two "junior Caesars," Galerius and Constantius, who would take power when he retired. This did not work, and by 324 Constantine (his English name) was Emperor of the whole Empire.

In 330, he dedicated the new city of Constantinople, on the site of the old Byzantium, to be the "New Rome," the capital in the East where the Emperor had to spend most of the time. It was modeled on Rome, with a Senate and free grain for the citizens, but there were no great temples in it, for Constantine had already chosen Christianity for his personal religion, although he was only baptized on his deathbed in 337. After him, the supremacy of Christianity in the Empire was almost guaranteed, although Julian 'the Apostate' (360-3) made one last attempt to bring back the old paganism. Theodosius became emperor in 379 and only died in 395. It was during his reign that Christianity became the official religion and, especially from 391, many laws were passed that gradually closed down the 'pagan' temples.

Before Constantine, many emperors had tried to find a mythical basis for their authority in religion. It was Constantine who realized that the emperor could be seen as the earthly representative of the heavenly Lord found in the Christian Bible. In 282, Carus had declared that the emperor was Dominus (Lord), not merely princeps (first). Aurelian (270-5) had gone farther by proclaiming himself dominus et deus, Lord and god, and under Constantine the imperial liturgy was finally organized as it continued at Constantinople until 1453. The emperor was considered to be sacred; he dressed in purple and gold vestments similar to those of priests, with incense before him, and all approaching had to fall prostrate before him.

The economical and political structure of the Empire gradually grew weaker and the main place of new vigor was the Church as it confronted its task of evangelizing the Empire. Already in 325, Constantine had presided over a Council of the Church's bishops at Nicaea, in Turkey, asking them to overcome their doctrinal disagreements, centered on the so-called Arian heresy. This combination of Church and State marks one beginning of the Middle Ages. Most of the great writers of this age are found in the Church: Ambrose, Jerome, Hilary, Augustine, Athanasius, John Chrysostom, Gregory of Nazianzus, Basil. Christianity spread quickly

In the deserts of Syria and Egypt, groups of men and women, fearing the corruptions of urban life, began to live alone as hermits or together in cenobitic communities, in lives consecrated entirely to God in prayer. Their single-minded consecration to God was expressed by the Greek word monos (single, one) and this is the origin of the English word 'monk'. The monastic life had begun, and would later yield the European monasteries whose libraries were to be the key to the survival of Roman literary culture during the coming Dark Age.

By about 404 the Roman legions left Britain to help defend Italy and after about 450 its eastern regions began to be occupied by new settlers: Saxons, Angles, Jutes from North Germany. Visigoths, Franks (who gave their name to France) and Burgundians, all Germanic, occupied much of Gaul, where they learned to speak the current form of Latin, that was to become French. In 410, the Gothic leader Alaric captured Rome and sacked it, marking the virtual end of the Roman Empire in the West. From far away to the East, the Huns had been advancing westwards for centuries. Under the leadership of Attila the Huns advanced into Gaul and Italy, sacking Rome in 452. Suddenly Attila died and the Huns disappeared from history.

The Vandal king Gaeseric again plundered Rome in 455, and from this time on, Italy became the scene of Ostrogothic (Lombard) kingdoms whose rulers acknowledged the Emperor in Constantinople and did as they wished. They used colloquial forms of Latin (romanice) and followed Roman laws, customs and culture. The Church continued to use the strict Latin language (grammatica), and in many cases was the only place in which writing was practiced, while the ordinary population developed new, relaxed forms of talking that became Italian, Spanish, French.

Slowly a new dynasty arose in northern Gaul, tracing its beginning from the Frankish leader Clovis (466 - 511) who made Paris his capital, became a Christian and extended his rule over all of what had been Gaul and was now becoming France. This 'Merovingian' dynasty ruled until they were ousted in 751. Pepin was crowned king, and when he died in 768, his son Charles (742-814) succeeded him as the greatest figure of the Carolingian Dynasty. He extended his kingdom to include vast areas of northern Germany, and also fought the Islamic Moors in northern Spain. In 800, on Christmas Day, Charles was crowned by the Pope in St. Peter's church at Rome as the new Holy Roman Emperor, but his throne was in Aachen, in Northern Germany; he is better known as Charlemagne.

The region between the Sinai Peninsula and Lebanon, known by many names, as Israel, Canaan, the Holy Land, Palestine, has no clear natural frontiers. The River Jordan, rising in what is now called Lebanon and flowing directly South, runs through the middle, parallel to the Mediterranean coast, southward through the lake called the Sea of Galilee(or Lake of Gennesareth) and on down into the Dead Sea where its waters evaporate, leaving the Dead Sea so charged with salts that nothing can grow near it, whence its name. The Dead Sea is far below sea-level.

Almost all the events of the Bible stories happen in towns lying to the West, between the Jordan and the sea. Jerusalem lies west of the point where the Jordan enters the Dead Sea. The Bible stories have two main centers, especially in New Testament times, one the area around Jerusalem, called Judea or Judah, from which comes the word "Jew", the other the area to the west of the Sea of Galilee, called Galilee. Between these lies the area called Samaria.

Most of the Holy Land is now rocky and not very fertile, but in Bible times it seemed less arid ("a land flowing with milk and honey"). The Jordan is a small river, of no importance for transportation though useful for irrigation. Before the small groups of families (tribes) calling themselves "the Children of Israel" took control of the land, it was called Canaan and in recent times, before the creation of the modern state of Israel, the land was called Palestine. To the South stretches the great desert of Sinai, between Israel and Egypt, caught between the two branches of the Red Sea.

【Early History: The Patriarchs】

In the first book of the Bible, *Genesis* (meaning beginning, origin), we see nomadic figures moving across the empty spaces of the Middle East between Mesopotamia and the Mediterranean regions. Especially we see a particular family, with proper names: Abraham, his son Isaac, his son Jacob(who is also called Israel, whence the name of the people"the children of Israel"). In the Bronze Age period between 2000 and 1500, semi-nomadic Amorites were coming down from the Syrian deserts into the fertile lands of Canaan, as well as across into Assyria. Among them archaeologists have found names such as Abram, Jacob, Levi, Benjamin. Their flocks of sheep were their main wealth, but they also had some interest in farming; this is the life-style of the "patriarchs" (fathers). These first fathers of the future tribes of Israel were Arameans, people speaking various Semitic languages.

Movements of population brought members of these "foreign" tribes down into Egypt, where they took power as the Hyksos(foreign rulers), and controlled Egypt from 1720-1580, when the Egyptians threw them out and asserted their own power as far as the Euphrates. This control by Egypt was reaffirmed by Rameses II around 1300, and after a campaign in Canaan in about 1230, his successor could write "Israel is laid waste", the first historical use of the name in the sense of a place inhabited by a specific group of people known as Israel.

【Moses and the Exodus】

After these victories, the Egyptians used more and more Semitic slaves and prisoners-of-war in their extensive new building projects, a kind of sub-proletariate they called "*apiru*", a word also found in Mesopotamia as "Habiru", meaning low-class mercenaries or slaves from the poor nomads; it is probably the origin of the word "Hebrew".

The well-known story of Moses(the name is Egyptian) who leads a group of escaping Semitic slaves out of Egypt *(Exodus)* and through the Sinai wilderness is rooted here. This group is shown as united, although the people are of various family-origins, by the action of a tribal god with the four-consonant name YHWH (*Yahweh-el*), but the name was rarely spoken, he was called *Elohim*, the Lord the familiar form "Jehovah" comes from a confusion, because the Hebrew Old Testament writes the vowels for *Elohim* over the Tetragrammaton.

For the next two centuries this original group of families, joined by others living in the hills of Canaan who accepted the same faith in the Lord, fought to take control of the Canaanite villages in the fertile areas near the Jordan. They were an amphictyony, a league united by a conviction that the Lord had established a special covenant with them. Here they found themselves confronted with the Philistine problem. These were "People of the Sea" whom Rameses III had driven out of Egypt and who had settled on the coast of Canaan around 1150. They may have come originally from Greece, their culture was partly

Mycenaean, and Homer mentions people with a similar name. They were stronger than Israel, partly because they had learned to make iron weapons, and in 1050 they defeated Israel and even captured the Ark of the Covenant(a wooden box or throne symbolizing the Lord's presence with Israel). The present name "Palestine" is derived from "Philistine".

【The Jerusalem Kingdom】

About 1000 B.C., it became clear to the religious leader (prophet) Samuel that the future of the amphictyony was in danger and that a strong king was needed to unite and lead the different families (tribes) living in Canaan that considered themselves to have been called by the Lord YHWH (*Yahweh-el*) to take control of the land. The modern state of Israel still bases its existence on this notion of a Promised Land given them by God. Until now there had been no social organization beyond that of individual extended families, each with their elder patriarch. Some felt that the Lord was Israel's king and that no other leader was needed.

After a first attempt with Saul that failed, in about 1012 David became the new king, first in the South, and crushed the Philistines. He was accepted by the remaining Canaanite populations, and imposed his rule so strongly that the surrounding peoples recognized his control over the whole land. Finally, he made the Canaanite city of Jerusalem his new capital, the center of the Covenant, and so unifying the various groups and tribes. David's forty years of kingship (1012 - 972) were partly inspired by the forms of divine kingship found in Mesopotamia, adapted to Israel's unique vision of a God who saves in history through his anointed servants.

David's son, Solomon, (ruled 972 - 931) made Israel part of the Mediterranean world by joining forces with the Phoenicians in commerce, by adopting much of their culture and by building a Temple at Jerusalem in Canaanite style, using Phoenician building techniques. Solomon's court was extremely sophisticated artistically and culturally. In this time orders were given to record in writing all the stories of Israel's origins that until then had only been transmitted orally, the writing of the Bible had begun. Some of the earliest texts in *Genesis* were written at this time, including the familiar story of Paradise, the Temptation of Eve by the serpent, and the Fall, by an individual writer often known as the Yahwist. All animal sacrifices were forbidden outside the new Jerusalem Temple, as well, so centralizing the religious life.

After Solomon died, however, the nation divided, there was much conflict and the tribes of the North established the Kingdom of Israel centered on the city of Samaria, while those of the South continued in Jerusalem, the center of the Kingdom of Judah. In 722, the Assyrians destroyed Samaria (and Damascus in Syria), and deported the people; the Northern Kingdom ceased to exist.

【Exile and Return】

For one thousand years, after Hammurabi had consolidated the unity of the Assyrian Empire, the main concern had been survival in a way of life close to that found in the Bible stories about Abraham and the patriarchs. Then, after the year 900, new energy brings the Assyrians into the Bible stories of the history of Judah, with wars and treaties involving kings such as Sennacherib (705-681).

Babylon was burned in 648, in response to a regionalistic uprising against the Assyrian kings, so the local citizens called in the Medes (who were Indo-Europeans) and in 612 Nineveh fell to the new dynasty. Under Nebuchadrezzar II (605-561) there was war with Egypt and invasion of Palestine. In 598the people around Jerusalem (Judah) rebelled, the king and 3000 citizens were taken back to Mesopotamia. When the survivors rebelled again in 589, Nebuchadrezzar (also known as Nebuchadnezzar, reigned 605 - 561) destroyed Jerusalem after a siege which lasted until 587.

This marks the beginning of the Exile, a vital time in Israel's history, for the Jewish exiles were not dispersed among the population of Mesopotamia; they continued to live close together. Their special religion served as a uniting force, and while studying the written "scriptures" (writings) they had brought with them, rewriting other records, and so composing the core of the Jewish Bible (called the Old Testament by Christians) they waited for the Lord of their past history to save them as he had saved their forefathers from Egypt. Since the Lord had always acted in history through human agents, and not by some kind of divine intervention, it was no great surprise when the long-awaited liberation from Exile and return to Jerusalem came from the Persian king Cyrus in 536, after his conquest of Babylon.

There they rebuilt the Jerusalem Temple, which was rededicated in 516. Only later, around 445, did they rebuild the city walls. Almost two generations had lived and died away from the "Holy Land", yet they had forgotten nothing of their faith. This miraculous return from

Exile and apparent disaster did not mean that Judah was able to become an independent state. Like Egypt, it remained part of the Persian zone of influence until the campaigns of Alexander the Great changed the face of the region. After that, the Jews were ruled by either the Ptolemies of Egypt or the Seleucids in Syrian Antioch.

The Bible: The Old Testament

While all Christians read the same New Testament, different churches read different forms of the Old Testament. The reason for this goes back to the origins of the Church. At the very beginning, the Easter message was "The Risen Jesus is Messiah and Lord." The first task was to convince the Jews that Jesus was the promised Messiah, that his sufferings and death had been foretold by Israel's prophets in the Scriptures. That demanded a close reading of the Jewish Scriptures, and a re-interpretation of them, since the Jews had mostly been expecting a celestial leader to come as Messiah, a new David who would throw out the Romans and re-establish Jerusalem as the City of God.

The thought of Paul, in particular, on the distinction between Law and Grace led the early Church ever farther away from Judaism as the Church opened more and more to people who had never had any contact with Jewish thought. It seemed that in Jesus, God had established a completely new 'Covenant' with humanity, one which not only fulfilled but virtually replaced the Covenant and laws received by Moses recorded in the Jewish Scriptures, that was limited essentially to Jews and those who chose to join them. Slowly the collection of fundamental Christian writings, the four Gospels, the Letters by Paul and other Apostles, came to be seen as the record of this 'New Covenant'; the Latin for 'Covenant' is testamentum and so it was only natural for the holy Scriptures of the Jews to receive the name 'Old Testament' by contrast to the 'New Testament'. It is, however, a name which Jews feel to be dismissive and therefore insulting.

The Hellenic (Greek-speaking) Jews and their disciples, who formed the bulk of the first generation of Christians, read the Jewish Scriptures in a Greek version, the Septuagint. Here they found all the books written in Hebrew translated into Greek, but also they found translations of some books first written in the Aramaic language spoken by the Jews after the Exile, and some books that were probably even originally composed in Greek, or the Hebrew originals have been lost. There was no finalized "canon" of exactly which books formed the "Holy Scriptures." The Septuagint, and its Latin parallel the "Vulgate", was the Old Testament of all Christians until the 16th century.

The Jews, after the destruction of Jerusalem, lived scattered in Diaspora, fiercely preserving their identity in a hostile world. The Hellenic world passed away, and other times came. Certain Jewish families (the Massoretes) were charged with the transmission of the Scriptures, and copies of the Hebrew books of the Bible were carefully made (the text itself was holy, every letter of it) and passed down by them from generation to generation. These families felt that the Bible could only be truly God's holy word in the Hebrew text. They therefore did not transmit the non-Hebrew works included in the Septuagint.

The Christian scholars of the German Renaissance (c.1500), Reuchlin and others, who sat down to learn Hebrew from the Jewish Rabbis (teachers) living in Europe, received from them the text of their Hebrew

Bible, and felt that this represented the "original" form, which the Septuagint had "corrupted" in some way. They set aside the parts of the Old Testament that were not found in the Hebrew Bible, calling them "Apocrypha" (meaning "hidden writings"), although the Church had been reading them from the very beginning of its history as integral parts of the Bible. Until today, the Catholic and Orthodox churches consider the "canon"(authorized list) of Scriptures to include the books of the Septuagint, whether written in Hebrew or not, while the Protestant churches exclude the Apocryphal books from their Bibles, or put them in a separate section. The order of the books in the Old Testament also varies, for the same reason.

【The Books of the Old Testament】

The first five books of the Bible are called the Pentateuch, or the Five Books of Moses (because traditionally they were said to have all been written by Moses). In the New Testament they are known as "The Law", the "Torah"; for Jews this is the most sacred part of the Bible. The English names given to the different books of the Pentateuch are mostly from the Latin; as we shall see, the divisions into books are often determined by the size of scrolls rather than by the contents.

【Genesis】

Chapter 1:1-2:3 offers a formal, theological narrative of the Creation of all things, all creatures, by God, an expression of the unity of creation and of the universal power of God. The basic structure of the narrative is that of the seven-day week. Seven was a sacred number, and the week was the fundamental unit of the Hebrew calendar.

The story is clearly designed to be a 'scientific' account, in the Aristotelian manner, emphasizing the unity of the Many by grouping things within broad general categories. The living creatures are introduced in a hierarchy determined by the way in which they reproduce; first come plants with seeds and fruit, then the egg-laying fish and birds, then the mammals, and finally humans, who are recognized as mammals by being created on the sixth day. The Creation ends on the Sabbath, the resting from work on the seventh day (Saturday). Since Sunday, the "first day of the (new) week", was the day of Jesus' Resurrection, it became the day when Christians rest and attend worship. It is not the Old Testament Sabbath.

1. In the beginning God created the heavens and the earth.
Now the earth was formless and empty,
darkness was over the surface of the deep,
and the Spirit of God was hovering over the waters.
And God said, "Let there be light"
and there was light.
God saw that the light was good
and he separated the light from the darkness.
God called the light "day"
and the darkness he called "night".
And there was evening, and there was morning
the first day.

6. And God said, "Let there be an expanse between the waters
to separate water from water."
So God made the expanse
and separated the water below from the water above.
And it was so.
God called the expanse "sky."
And there was evening, and there was morning the second day.

9. And God said, "Let the water under the sky be gathered together
and let dry ground appear."
And it was so.
God called the dry ground "land"
and the gathered waters he called "seas "
And God saw that it was good.
Then God said, "Let the land produce vegetation:
seed-bearing plants, and trees on the land
that bear fruit with seeds in it, according to their various kinds."
And it was so.
The land produced vegetation:
plants bearing seeds according to their kinds.
And trees bearing fruit with seed in it according to their kinds.
And God saw that it was good.
And there was evening and there was morning
the third day.

14. And God said, "Let there be lights in the expanse of the sky

to separate the day from the night;
and let them serve as signs to mark seasons and days and years,
and let them be lights in the expanse of the sky
to give light on the earth."
And it was so.
God made two great lights,
the greater light to govern the day
and the lesser light to govern the night.
He also made the stars.
God set them in the expanse of the sky
to give light on the earth to govern the day and the night,
and to separate light from darkness.
And God saw that it was good.
And there was evening and there was morning
the fourth day.

20. And God said, "Let the water teem with living creatures,
and let birds fly above the earth across the expanse of the sky."
So God created the great creatures of the sea
and every living, moving thing with which the water teems,
according to their kinds,
and every winged bird according to its kind.
And God saw that it was good.
God blessed them and said,
"Be fruitful and increase in number and fill the water in the seas,
and let the birds increase on the earth."

And there was evening and there was morning
the fifth day.

24. And God said, "Let the land produce living creatures
according to their kinds:
livestock, creatures that move along the ground,
and wild animals, each according to its kind."
And it was so.
God made the wild animals according to their kinds,
the livestock according to their kinds,
and all the creatures that move along the ground
according to their kinds.
And God saw that it was good.

26. Then God said, "Let us make man in our image, in our likeness,
and let them rule over the fish of the sea and the birds of the air,
over the livestock, over all the wild animals of the earth,
and over all the creatures that move along the ground."
So God created man in his own image,
in the image of God he created him,
male and female he created them.
God blessed them and said to them,
"Be fruitful and increase in number; fill the earth and subdue it.
Rule over the fish of the sea and the birds of the air,
and over every living creature that moves on the ground."
Then God said,

41. I give you every seed-bearing plant on the face of the whole earth
and every tree that has fruit with seed in it.
They will be yours for food.
And to all the beasts of the earth
and all the birds of the air
and all the creatures that move on the ground,
everything that has the breath of life in it
I give every green plant for food." And it was so.
God saw all that he had made
and it was very good.
And there was evening and there was morning
the sixth day.

(Chapter 2)
Thus the heavens and the earth were completed in all their vast array.
By the seventh day God had finished the work he had been doing;
so on the seventh day he rested from all his work.
And God blessed the seventh day and made it holy,
because on it he rested from all the work of creating that he had done.

Chapter 2:4-3:end contain the other, older story of the creation of humanity, with the symbolic names Adam (Man) and Eve (Living), their life in "Paradise" (garden) with visits from YHWH (the name is not used in Chapter 1), the story of the Tree of the knowledge of good and evil, the temptation of Eve, the Fall, the punishment and the Expulsion from the Garden. A mysterious story, combining many elements, not at all a "full explanation" or a "myth" in the usual sense. It stands at the beginning of the Bible as an expression of a truth about humanity: people do not do what they know to be God's will, and the result is unhappiness, suffering, hardship.

This is the account of the heavens and the earth when they were created. When the LORD God made the earth and the heavens, no shrub of the field had yet appeared on the earth and no plant of the field had yet sprung up; the LORD God had not sent rain on the earth and there was no man to work the ground, but streams came up from the earth and watered the whole surface of the ground. And the LORD God formed a man (Adam) from the dust of the ground and breathed into his nostrils the breath of life, and he became a living being.

Now the LORD God had planted a garden in the east, in Eden; and there he put the man he had formed. And the Lord God made all kinds of trees grow out of the ground, trees that were pleasing to the eye and good for food. In the middle of the garden were the tree of life and the tree of the knowledge of good and evil ....

(15) The LORD God took Adam and put him in the Garden of Eden to work it and take care of it. And the LORD God commanded the man, "You are free to eat from any tree in the garden; but you must not eat from the tree of the knowledge of good and evil for when you eat of it you will surely die."

The LORD God said, "It is not good for the man to be alone. I will make a helper suitable for him....... (21) So the Lord God caused the man to fall into a deep sleep, and while he was sleeping, he took one of the man's ribs and closed up the place with flesh. Then the LORD God made a woman from the rib he had taken out of the man, and he brought her to the man ....

(25) The man and his wife were both naked, and they felt no shame.

Chapter 3: The Fall

Now the serpent was more crafty than any of the wild animals the LORD God had made. He said to the woman, "Did God really say You must not eat from any tree in the garden?"

The woman said to the serpent, "We may eat fruit from the trees in the garden, but God did say, 'You must not eat fruit from the tree that is in the middle of the garden, and you must not touch it, or you will die.'"

"You will not surely die," the serpent said to the woman. "For God knows that when you eat it your eyes will be opened, and you will be like God, knowing good and evil."

When the woman saw that the fruit of the tree was good for food and pleasing to the eye, and also desirable for gaining wisdom, she took some and ate it She also gave some to her husband, who was with her, and he ate it. Then the eyes of both of them were opened, and they realized that they were naked; so they sewed fig leaves together and made coverings for themselves. Then the man and his wife heard the sound of the LORD God as he was walking in the garden in the cool of the day, and they hid from the LORD God among the trees of the garden. But the LORD God called to the man, "Adam, where are you?" He answered, "I heard you in the garden, and I was afraid because I was naked; so I hid."

And he said, "Who told you that you were naked? Have you eaten from the tree that -1 commanded you not to eat from?"

Adam said, "The woman you put here with me, she gave me some fruit from the tree, and I ate it." Then the LORD God said to the woman, "What is this you have done?" The woman said, "The serpent deceived me, and I ate."....

So the LORD God banished him from the Garden of Eden to work the ground from which he had been taken. After he drove the man out, he placed on the east side of the Garden of Eden cherubim and a flaming sword flashing back and forth to guard the way to the tree of life.

In Chapter 5 there are strange lists of people reported to have lived for 900 years, the oldest being Methuselah, who has become proverbial.

Chapter 6:1-9:17 contains the epic of Noah, a story which is close to that found in Mesopotamia, (see the Gilgamesh Flood Myth in Chapter 1) where terrible floods were very common. It should be seen as a symbolic new beginning offered to humanity by God, the hope exists that even the worst disaster is not the end of God's love and promises. Noah is shown as a man of faith, and a craftsman able to build the Ark, but not as an extraordinary person, Noah is a normal human being, the Bible is not interested in the "heroic".

In Chapter 10 there are lists of strange tribes, records of places: the Bible is from the beginning anchored in a culture, a history, a specific geography, not ours. It expresses its message in a universal context. This is the meaning of what follows.

Chapter 11:1-9, the story of the Tower of Babel, an allegory of the multiplicity of languages by which people are divided, both a blessing and a curse. Here, as in the stories about Eve and Noah, we must note that humor is not absent.

With the end of Chapter 11 we enter a new stage in the narrative of Israel's past. What had been told until now applied to all humanity, was not linked to "history" in the way that what follows claims to be. Now the Bible begins the history of salvation worked out in reality, not myth, through faithful individuals and families, the Patriarchs (fathers). This is essentially a family epic, in prose, preserving many memories of an early period in human history when life was nomadic and pastoral, and here too there is none of the heroic exaggeration of other cultures. The only "extraordinary" thing noted about Abraham, for example, is his trust in God.

Abraham, Isaac and Jacob, the Patriarchs, are seen as the founding fathers of the families (tribes) making up the later Amphictyony of Israel. Israel is a later name given to Jacob. As in all such foundation histories, the symbolic is mixed with the historical. Most important, there is here nothing of the usual Myth, no unions with gods, no supernatural origin, only the appearance of a group of people seeing itself as being in a special relationship with God, who has made them a promise of blessings. The meeting with God remains mysterious.

Chapter 12:1-7, the beginning of the Abraham story, expresses the promise of God in a very undramatic way, with no details about how God appeared. Abraham sets out, returning to the nomadic life which was already being replaced by sedentary farming. Abraham's setting out is seen as a expression of his trust in God, who has promised him another life in another place.

In the saga of Abraham, there are many adventures, in which he is sometimes seen meeting God in humble ways (chapter 18), and even arguing with him, making God change his mind (chapter 18:25-end). For a long time Abraham has no son, there is the puzzle of who will inherit the promise. Then, very late, God enables him to have a son, Isaac.

Chapter 22:1-18, tells how God "tests" Abraham, ordering him to sacrifice his only son, Isaac. Child sacrifice was common in the tribes of Canaan, this story is designed to discourage it, but later the Church saw in it a "type" of the love of God who was ready to give up his only Son. "Typology" involves finding a new meaning in a story by events happening later, so that events of the Old Testament are found to be "allegories" of what happens when Jesus comes.

The last part of Genesis (chapters 37-50) consists of another literary type, an adventure story or popular romance in which a person is separated from his family, becomes very powerful, then confronts the family in this new position; once the relationship is discovered, there is reconciliation. The story of Joseph, sold by his brothers into slavery in Egypt where he becomes the servant of Pharaoh thanks to his interpretation of dreams, is one of the world's first "comic" stories. This story is remarkable, both by its "change in fortunes" themes and by the emotionally touching scenes involving Benjamin (the youngest son) and the old father Jacob. It is extremely well structured. The story is put here to explain why the "children of Israel" were in Egypt.

【Exodus】

For Israel, the memory of the central events of Exodus (Passover and escape from slavery in Egypt) was the basis of their religious and national existence. Unlike any other nation, the stories on which Israel's religion was based were not Fables but History, and even when centuries of "oral transmission" have added some fabulous details, the basic historical nature of the Exodus epic is clear.

Moses comes at a moment when the "Habiru" in Egypt are most totally oppressed, exploited and desperate. Because God is with him, he is able to lead those who follow him out on a journey reflecting that undertaken by Abraham. It is only when the risk has been taken that God appears to them all at Sinai and establishes the "Covenant" which binds all the families involved into a single group with a united religion.

Moses is often seen as a magician, especially in the rather grim competitions of the Plagues sent on Egypt (chapters 7-11); but the early story of the Burning Bush (chapter 3) is central, expressing the special vocation of Moses to whom the Lord (YHWH) reveals his Name. In Israel, the name is thought to express a person's essential being; here, the ancient tribal god's name YHWH is given a deeper meaning by being linked to the Hebrew verb "to be". With Moses, "theophany" becomes more concrete than in the stories of Genesis. It becomes the starting-point of a new history.

Chapter 12, the story of the Passover, when the Egyptian Pharaoh at last agrees to let the people go, marks a change from "romantic" to "cultic." The events in Egypt are told in a popular way, with little reflection as to why all these plagues are necessary; but the passover meal is not a "story" but a fact of every Jew's life, until today. Originally a springtime festival before the shepherds set out for the summer pastures, the Passover is kept at the full moon of the first month (March-April). The family is together at home, the Passover lamb is sacrificed, but no bone is broken, there is a special ritual of thanksgiving prayers before and during the meal, at which "unleavened bread" is eaten, and a number of cups of wine are shared. Then the head of the family relates the Saving Deeds of the Lord so that the children will remember them. "Salvation" in the Old Testament means "being saved" from some quite concrete difficulty or danger, usually as a nation (Israel). In the centuries of Diaspora, the Jewish hope was kept alive by the final greeting, "Next year in Jerusalem."

This Passover event gave the Christian church important elements. Jesus, dying on the Cross just before the feast of Passover, became the "real" Lamb of God, the "sacrifice" that saved all. The meal of the Passover that Jesus shared with his companions at his Last Supper became the regular Christian celebration, celebrated every week as a memorial of the Resurrection, with the cup of wine and the unleavened bread forming the basic materials of the Mass (Eucharist, Lord's Supper). Some of the words said daily at Mass are from the ritual of the Passover ("Lift up you hearts", "Holy, holy, holy.")

The crossing of the Red Sea (or more probably 'Reed Sea', a marshy area along the route from Egypt to Sinai) is told in chapter 14, with rather less drama than Hollywood suggests, and the people begin their journey through the desert. The Old Testament dislikes idealization, the Israelites in the desert are extremely human in their regret for the "fleshpots of Egypt", the easy life of days gone by. The love of the Lord is shown in the gifts of Manna and quails, his feeding of people who without him would have died.

Chapter 19 brings them to Sinai, and Moses goes up the mountain to meet with God and receive the Ten Commandments. These are listed at the beginning of Chapter 20, as the introduction to the many laws listed in the chapters following:

And God spoke all these words: "I am the LORD your God, who brought you out of Egypt, out of the land of slavery. You shall have no other gods before me.

"You shall not make for yourself an idol in the form of anything in heaven above or on the earth beneath or in the waters below. You shall not bow down to them or worship them; for I, the LORD your God, am a jealous God, punishing the children for the sin of the fathers to the third and fourth generation of those who hate me, but showing love to a thousand [generations] of those who love me and keep my commandments.

"You shall not misuse the name of the LORD your God, for the LORD will not hold anyone guiltless who misuses his name.

"Remember the Sabbath day by keeping it holy. Six days you shall labor and do all your work, but the seventh day is a Sabbath to the LORD your God. On it you shall not do any work, neither you, nor your son or daughter, nor your manservant or maidservant, nor your animals, nor the alien within your gates. For in six days the LORD made the heavens and the earth, the sea, and all that is in them, but he rested on the seventh day. Therefore the LORD blessed the Sabbath day and made it holy.

"Honor your father and your mother, so that you may live long in the land the LORD your God is giving you.

"You shall not murder.

"You shall not commit adultery.

"You shall not steal.

"You shall not give false testimony against your neighbor.

"You shall not covet your neighbor's house. You shall not covet your neighbor's wife, or his manservant or maidservant, his ox or donkey, or anything that belongs to your neighbor."

The Covenant, the Contract between God and his People, Israel, was expressed after Solomon in the daily sacrifices offered by Levites (priests from the tribe Levi) in the name of the People in the great Temple at Jerusalem. This is represented by the detailed cultic laws contained in the chapters which follow.

The only other narrative of the wanderings in the desert in Exodus is that of chapter 32, the story of the Golden Calf, still today a popular symbol for the ease with which people set up false "idols" and run after them. After this disaster, there comes a renewal of the Covenant and a new set of laws. God, clearly, does not give up.

【The Rest of the Pentateuch】

Originally, there were not clear divisions between all these stories, but the size of the scrolls on which they could be written made it necessary to divide them. The last book of the Pentateuch, Deuteronomy (the second Law), comes after lists of laws making up Leviticus, and many varying stories about the life in the desert (Numbers). Deuteronomy is much easier to read, it is certainly written by a unifying author. It is in the form of Moses' last declarations, in which he reminds Israel of all God's saving mercies and warns them of the disasters that will come if they do not keep the commandments and worship the Lord seriously. This theme is made poignant by the fact that this book was discovered and read in 622, not long before the destruction of Jerusalem, but too late for much to be done. It was probably written in much its present form under Hezekiah (c. 700) using the old stories handed down from the time of the desert and of the Exodus itself (1300-1200?).

【Early History of Israel】

The books Joshua and Judges tell the early history of the Israelites' invasion and occupation of Canaan. These stories are often heroic, and popular. They oversimplify reality, but always from the point of view of faith. The basic pattern is God-centered, he leads the people by inspired leaders; when the people fail to obey God or his leaders ("Judges" means inspired leaders) they get into trouble. They then see their mistake, repent, and the Covenant is renewed.

Typical, and most famous, of these stories is that of Samson (Judges 13-16) who is a universal figure, brave, weak about women, witty. His capture by Delilah has inspired several films; his final imprisonment and death are the subject of Milton's only tragedy, "Samson Agonistes."

After the beautiful little romantic narrative of Ruth, designed to introduce the story of David, we come to more history, of a more familiar, official kind. The books of Samuel (only divided because of the size of scrolls, again) tell how Israel ceased to be a prehistoric federation of tribes and became a political monarchy. The transition from nomadic to settled life, from patriarchal informality to kingship, from scattered sanctuaries to the Temple, all came together and culminate in the reigns of David and Solomon.

【Kingship】

The two Books of Samuel begin with the figure of Samuel, called a "prophet" but better seen as a form of "Judge." It is his task to introduce the king, this being seen as a better constitutional form for the newly unified tribes and peoples of Canaan. They end with David as king, after telling the dramatic events of the "reign" of Saul, his psychological breakdown, and replacement by the young hero who as a young man had faced Goliath and killed him with a stone (chapter 17).

Nothing in the Bible can equal these books for their "human interest", they read like a novel, full of adultery and murder, rape and treachery, pride and folly. David himself is a man of passion, cruelty and despair. The main religious theme in these books is that of God's choice of individuals; David is sinful, passionate, but he is God's "Anointed" (the word Christ, Messiah in Hebrew, means just that), the King who is responsible for leading God's People. David too is the inheritor of a promise, and for Christians Jesus is the fulfillment of that promise; that is why Jesus is born (in Luke's Gospel) in Bethlehem, the "city of David", into the family descended from David.

The two Books of Kings are also neither separate from each other nor separate from Samuel, which they continue. The first book tells the end of David's reign, and continues the history through all the kings of North and South until the destruction of Samaria in 722, and of Jerusalem in 587.

The theme here is not that of Samuel. The disasters are seen as the fault of the kings, who let the people go astray. But the Covenant and the Commandments continue; the code of Deuteronomy is clearly affirmed: one God to be worshiped at one Temple. The problems come from the introduction of foreign gods and cults, or from the worship of the Lord performed away from Jerusalem, especially in Samaria. The result is a moralizing reading of historical events, quite unique in its time. At the same time, stories are introduced about "prophets" who are men of holiness, in contrast to the king. Elijah and Elisha work miracles that are echoed in those of Jesus, they are true Men of God, although they are poor and they suffer. The message here is of hope in God's love, and these books must have been vital in the Exile, which they show is not the defeat of the Lord, but his vindication. God is holy, even if his People is not.

The two Books of Chronicles tell much the same history, from Adam until David in the form of genealogies, then in a highly edited historical narrative. The message here is again that God is one and that his Temple is in Jerusalem; probably this was intended to encourage the Jews returning from Exile to be careful not to repeat the sins of the past. The. story here serves to preach repentance and conversion.

This is continued in the two books which follow, Ezra and Nehemiah, originally part of Chronicles. They tell the story of the return from the Exile, thanks to Cyrus the Persian's edict (538), first of a group that rebuilt the Temple (rededicated in 515), then of others under Ezdra (458). Of course, many others had remained in Judah. Perhaps about 60-80,000 were in Babylon, another 30-40,000 remained in Judah. In

445 Nehemiah brought another group back to Jerusalem, and the city walls were rebuilt and society reorganized according to the old ideas. Finally there were celebrations of the Covenant and repentance in 425.

These books are different from the previous histories, in that they are written close to the events they describe, they are vital evidence for historians. But their message is religious. In the Exile, Israel had become aware of itself in a new way. No longer simply a population, but a "church" with a Bible (much had been written just before the Exile, most of the other parts were composed in nearly their present form during or just after the Exile). Many of those returning were not moved by religious ideals, so that the writers and religious leaders had to try to move them, inspire them. There is no longer an independent state of Judah, even. Here is the birthplace of "Judaism", the Jewish identity that can survive centuries of persecution and exile; the system that Jesus confronts in the new Testament, with the "Scribes" (experts in God's Law) and the "Sanhedrin" (Council of Elders with administrative power).

This section of the Bible is completed by short, late, "romances" of Tobit, Judith, Esther, mostly written in Greek.

【Poetry: Wisdom Literature】

Seven books are grouped to form the poetry of Israel, between the historical books and the Prophets. In Jewish and Protestant Bibles these are reduced to five, since The Wisdom of Solomon and Sirach (Ecclesiasticus) are not accepted, one because it is written in Greek, the other because it was composed too late to be included in the "sacred" texts. Both are remarkable works and well worth reading.

【Job】

The Book of Job is one of the great books of world literature, quite unique in the Bible and read by people who would never look at any other part of the Judaeo-Christian tradition. It starts and ends with prose narratives describing an overturn of Fortune; Job has everything, sons, wealth, flocks, servants, and suddenly he loses it all. At the end, Fortune returns and everything is restored. The main substance, though, lies in the poetry between, dialogues and monologues in which Job and his companions, then God himself, debate the question "why do the innocent suffer?"

This was a familiar question, across Mesopotamia and Egypt similar debates are found, and in the prophets and Psalms too the question is raised. But this book, whose author is nameless but who seems identified by suffering with the gentile Job, goes much further in its challenge to conventional religion. Even the Proverbs, like the whole deuteronomic tradition, suggest that the person who obeys the Law of the Lord will be blessed with success, health and wealth, that suffering is a punishment for sin. Job simply stands there and objects that he has done no wrong, that death is a mystery, that as a human being he is entitled to some answers. In this, Job is more the first "Romantic Hero" than Prometheus could ever be.

Like the Platonic dialogues, though in a different way, Job teaches by not giving any solution. The friends of Job, in speeches presenting the "orthodox" arguments, are the original "Job's Comforters" (no comfort at all) and in the New Testament, the Epistle of James (5:11) mentions Job's "patience" which has also become proverbial, though not accurate. Even the imagined reply of God, when it finally comes in chapters 38-40, is not a reply but only a challenge to the limits of the human mind and physical power.

There is, God seems to say, no real explanation for human suffering. If there is, it is too difficult for humans. Instead, the Lord talks at length about the marvels of nature, the mysterious creatures known in Hebrew as Behemoth and Leviathan. Job simply submits to the superior Mystery and all his losses are restored. It was only the Cross and Passion of Jesus that finally offered believing humanity an insight into what the answer to Job's questions might be. Even then, the sense of suffering is not something that can be explained in words.

The poetry of Job's elegies on human destiny and frailty is sublime; the writers of the 18th century, very fond of the word "sublime", always explained it by referring to Job. William Blake, particularly, pondered Job's words and reflected them in his engravings and paintings.

【The 150 Psalms】

These are the "hymns" of Jewish worship. They were originally sung in the Temple during worship, they express some of the deepest religious feelings of God's People. They are greatly varied in theme. Some read as if they were deeply personal complaints, others are national celebrations or royal victory songs, some express deep trust in God, others ask questions, some demand vengeance or justice, many are laments in sickness and despair. They continue to be sung and prayed daily by many people. They have always been a main source for the Christian church's prayers and meditations. The numbering of the Psalms differs in the Hebrew and Greek versions, and therefore today in Catholic and Protestant versions, where the traditional Catholic numbering is mostly one behind that found in most Bibles.

The 22nd / 23rd Psalm is the most famous:

The Lord is my shepherd, I shall not lack.
He makes me lie down in green pastures,
he leads me beside still waters,
he restores my soul.
He guides me in the paths of righteousness
for his name's sake.
Though I walk through the valley of the shadow of death,
I will fear no evil
for you are with me;
your rod and staff
will comfort me.
You prepare a table before me
in the presence of my enemies.
You anoint my head with oil,
my cup overflows.
Surely goodness and mercy will follow me
all the days of my life,
and I will dwell in the house of the Lord for ever

According to Matthew, Jesus dies on the Cross quoting Psalm 22 "My God, my God, why have you forsaken me?" having fulfilled its prophetic descriptions of his crucifixion. Some Psalms, like the 118th / 119th are structured by the Hebrew alphabet; it is the longest and perhaps the most profound.

Traditionally, the author of the first Psalms was David, the greatest biblical poet and musician, and certain Psalms carry his name in their title, although it is not easy to find his hand in them. Most of the Psalms seem to have been written in their present form either during or after the Exile. The poetry of the Bible is best seen in the Psalm, with repeated parallelisms of a kind also found in the classical couplet.

The Proverbs must have originally been collections of traditional sayings, common in oral culture. To these have been added many artificially composed as a means of instructing young people in good living. Didactic intentions are common in the Bible. Some of the proverbs are most diverting, some compare well with the terseness of Greek epigrams. Proverbs already make the distinction between the Fool and the man of Wisdom which is much developed in the later books, such as the Wisdom of Solomon. There, the figure of Wisdom is developed in a personifying direction, becoming a companion of God in his creating Work as well as the guide of wise men. In the end, this personification of divine Wisdom is one aspect of the "Word" evoked by John at the beginning of his Gospel.

Ecclesiastes is a work that many have loved for its asperity; it is a companion of the book of Job in raising difficult questions, but it is more radically skeptical about human affairs. The book begins and ends with "Vanity", the emptiness of human business, and true Wisdom seems reserved for the melancholic on-looker who sees existence for what it really is. All life is seen as lying under the universal law of death, the writer/speaker (Ecclesiastes meaning "preacher") suggests that great detachment is necessary. He is a man of simplicity and faith, close to many modern satirical writers in their standpoint of ironic detachment. He is perhaps the first religious satirist.

The Song of Songs is the direct opposite. At the surface level, it is a series of erotic love poems in the form of exchanges between two shepherds, with the speakers difficult to disentangle. It claims to have been written by Solomon, which seems unlikely. It is marvelous poetry, but not at all religious in subject-matter. Therefore people have always read it as an Allegory, God being one of the lovers, Israel the other; then, after the coming of Christ, Christians said that it could be read typologically as a celebration of the love between Christ and the Church. Most people today simply read it for its unrestrained lyricism and sensual imagery.

【The Prophets】

For Jesus, the word "Bible" did not exist; he either talks of the "Scriptures" or the "Law and the Prophets." The Law was given by God, through Moses, the Prophets were the men sent from God to call Israel back from sin and point the right way forward. The prophet was always, then, a speaker, someone with a "message", a word from God. In all religions there are messages from the gods, oracles or signs. In Israel there were professional prophets from early times, probably, but the great prophets of the Bible are more like the Voice of Conscience than anything else. They are by nature dissidents and oppositionists.

The books called the Prophets are most complex because the prophets themselves did not usually write, but they had followers, disciples who made collections of their sayings and adventures. The books Isaiah and Jeremiah are especially long and complicated, it is almost impossible to pick them up and read them through with any real understanding.

The prophets' sayings were always uttered in a social, political context and always had some kind of inner drive forcing the prophet to express them. These are not ideas which the prophet happened to formulate by thinking, they are not the result of a rational process. That would not make them "the Word of the Lord." The prophets live in a special relationship with God, it is his Spirit who "inspires" (breathes into) them. We cannot imagine, then, the prophetic moment, we have only the word as it was later recorded. This is also often poetry.

The idea that a "prophet" is able to foretell the future is incorrect, he is first of all a "soothsayer" ('sooth' means truth). There soon arose, especially in the case of Jeremiah, conflicts about who was right, since the prophet often spoke out against the king and the governmental policy, he was often in a minority and taken for mad. Only future events would show who was right. Here the deuteronomic vision was important, the idea that a people could follow or go astray from the Way of the Lord. Prophecy is an attempt at social reform and purification, in the name of God. The tone may be denunciatory or hortatory.

Only in the early days of the Church, after the Resurrection and in the first inspiration of the Spirit, there was a real question about who Jesus was, how his life should be understood? The prophets were important for this, Isaiah especially was found to have "prophesied" about him, centuries before. Indeed, Jesus in the Gospels quotes from Isaiah more often than from any other book of the Scriptures. This Messianic theme, of which the prophets and their disciples must have been quite unconscious, gave a new dimension to Christians' readings of these books.

The name "prophet" is given to two different kinds of figures in the Old Testament. First, in the histories, we have Samuel, Elijah, Elisha, "men of God" who are set in contrast to the kings but who are not usually involved in giving messages. Second, behind the texts of the Prophetic books, we sense men of fire who cannot be silent in the face of looming disaster. They try to communicate their message in many ways, by many styles of speech but also by gestures, or by actions, so that their lives become prophecy.

【Isaiah】

This book is very complex, yet the richest in many ways. There are two main parts: chapters 1-39 and chapters 40-66, although chapters 56-66 also seem to stand apart. The first part seems to deal mostly with events in the years around 740-730. The prophet (Isaiah) tells of his vocation in a vision of God in chapter 6:

In the year that king Uzziah died, I saw the LORD seated on a throne, high and lifted up, and the train of his robe filled the temple. Above him were seraphs, each with six wings: With two wings they covered their faces, with two they covered their feet, with two they flew. And they called to one another: "Holy! Holy! Holy is the LORD Almighty; the whole earth is full of his glory." At the sound of their voices the doorposts and thresholds shook and the temple was filled with smoke.

"Woe is me!" I cried. "I am lost. For I am a man of unclean lips and I live among a people of unclean lips, and my eyes have seen the King, the LORD Almighty."

Then one of the seraphs flew to me with a live coal in his hand, which he had taken with tongs from the altar. With it he touched my mouth and said, "See, this has touched your lips; your guilt is taken away and your sin atoned for."

Then I heard the voice of the LORD saying, "Whom shall I send? And who will go for us? " And I said, "Here am I. Send me."

There are passages both before (chapter 5, the Parable of the Vine) and after (chapter 7-12, the coming of the child 'Emmanuel') which are echoed in the New Testament.

The person we can only call Deutero-Isaiah (Second Isaiah) must have lived in Babylon during the Exile and returned to Jerusalem with the first group, if chapters 56-66 are by the same person. The climax of his historical vision is the coming fall of Babylon (539) and the return of the exiles, so that the main theme is one of Consolation.

The style is highly poetic. Most important are the sections usually called The Songs of the Suffering Servant, in chapters 42:1-6, 49:1-7, and above all chapter 53.

He grew up like a tender shoot before us,
like a root out of dry ground.
He had no beauty or majesty to attract us to him,
nothing in his appearance that we should desire.
He was despised and rejected by men
a man of sorrows and acquainted with grief
Like one from whom people hide their faces he was despised,
and we esteemed him not.
He carried our infirmities
and bore our grief,
yet we considered him stricken by God,
struck down by him, and afflicted.
But he was pierced for our transgressions,
crushed for our iniquities;
the punishment that brought us peace was upon him
and by his wounds we are healed.

Here the Church was to find a key to the mystery of Jesus as a suffering Messiah, where Israel had looked for a triumphant one. These passages are in themselves mysterious, which helped the Church to turn them into Messianic typology. There are also many other magnificent passages, foretelling the joy of the Return from Exile and the universal mission of the future Israel (chapter 60). In chapters 63-4 Isaiah addresses the Lord as "our Father", which is not common before Jesus.

Important in the Second and Third Isaiah prophecies is the future perspective. The faith of Israel had been turned towards the past, the memory of Moses and Egypt, or of David. From this time on there is a future to be looked for, a Coming, a Day of the Lord "Behold, I will create new heavens and a new earth" (Isaiah 65:17). Many of these words have become familiar by their use in Handel's "Messiah." The rhythms of English are especially marked by the style of Isaiah, which is one of the highest in the whole Bible. It is the book that Jesus quotes from most frequently in the Gospels.

【Jeremiah】

The book of Jeremiah is almost as difficult to disentangle as Isaiah, since very many prophetic sayings of various origins and styles have been grouped under the name of the great Jeremiah. Jeremiah's own message and life can be found in scattered passages, where he stands out as a reluctant prophet, born in obscurity (chapter 1). His public career began when he preached in the Temple and at once provoked opposition (chapters 26-7). He lived at the time when the crisis of the Exile was approaching. King Josiah (640-609) had tried hard to restore the worship of the Lord in the Temple, especially after the finding of the scroll of the Law (parts of Deuteronomy) in the Temple in 622, but after Josiah was killed fighting the Egyptians, the reform was abandoned and injustice returned under Jehoiakim, whom Jeremiah began to criticize.

Jeremiah stands out as the "typical" prophet, proclaiming divine and moral absolutes and denouncing political or social abuses. He had to endure persecution, his life was in danger, but he refused to be silent and denounced those who "prophesied" what the powerful wanted to hear. During the last revolt of Jerusalem, (589-7), he recommended surrender to Babylon, and was thrown into prison. He bought land as a sign that he believed in a future for his people in Jerusalem, and after the fall of Jerusalem was taken to Egypt, not into the Babylonian Captivity, where he died, after writing to the exiles in Babylon.

The third of the "great" prophetic books is that of Ezekiel, who speaks to the Jews of the first deportation (597), before and after the final fall of Jerusalem. His tone is strong, partly because he has to struggle for the attention of people tempted to give up all hope. He has many visions to report, in a language much more tormented and mysterious than that of, say, Isaiah's vocation. It is interesting to compare the heavenly visions of Isaiah 6 and Ezekiel 1. He looks forward to a restoration of Israel with the Temple as the center of its life.

【The "Minor" Prophets】

The remaining books of the Old Testament are a collection of twelve or so prophetic books, together with the book of Daniel, and the history of the Maccabees (not in the Hebrew and Protestant Bible). Of these, Daniel and Jonas are the most familiar.

Daniel is divided into two parts, the first telling stories set in the time of the Exile, the second looking towards an "End of the World", an Apocalypse. Among the stories (not historical, the book of Daniel was written around 166 B.C.) we find that of Daniel in the Lions' Den (chapter 6), the Three Children in the Fiery Furnace (chapter 3), and Belshazzar's Feast (chapter 5). In all these, the power of Israel's God is stressed. In the remaining chapters (7-12) we have narratives of an "Apocalypse" (Apocalypse means unveiling), an End of Time in which God finally establishes his Kingdom, overturns the wicked and "raises up" the just. This book anticipates the Book of Revelations at the end of the New Testament, and both reflect attempts to deal with the difficulty of hoping for the best in a wicked world.

Jonas, like Daniel 1-6, is a fictional narrative. The story of the three days spent by the prophet in the belly of the whale has always appealed to the imagination.

【The Social Vision of the Prophets】

Historically, the prophets were speaking out before, during, and after the Exile (587 - 530 BC), which represents the disaster that justifies their warnings and tests their hopes. We may divide them into:

A. Pre-exilic Prophets

Amos, Hosea, First Isaiah, Micah, Zephania, Habakkuk.

B. Exilic Prophets

Jeremiah, Ezekiel, Second Isaiah.

C. Post-exilic Prophets

Third Isaiah, Zechariah, Malachi.

One main characteristic of all the above writings is the importance of "social justice" in the will of God. They were witnesses of deep corruption, of cheating, exploitation, cruelty. In Hebrew there are two words of great importance; one, mishpat (justice) is the result of a trial in which judges examine a situation of conflict and try to decide who is acting wrongly, who is in the right. It is allied to "human rights" because society always inclines to abuses of power, the weak are always being wronged by the rich and powerful. This is a "wrong relationship" and its opposite, a "right relationship" is what is covered by the second word, sedaga (righteousness). Israel existed in relationship, with God and with itself. The relationship with God was kept right by faithful worship and by observing the ritual laws; the relationship with God must, obviously, be reflected in the social relationships of God's People.

The poor and helpless ("orphans and widows") had a more than symbolic role in Israel. They were, from the texts in Exodus already, the sign and test of Israel's "godliness" (holiness). God's People was a "holy People", the weak and the strong together. If the strong exploit and hurt the weak, they are offending God; the weak, by definition, cannot exploit and hurt the rich and powerful. The Covenant with God was essentially a "Social Contract" with very clear consequences in society.

In the cities of Canaan, society was living a "market economy" and very quickly the prophets saw (they were "seers") the hypocrisy of "religious" people involved in making profits at the expense of the poor. In Athens, at about the same time, the result was revolution and tyranny. But in Israel, there was the additional factor of the invisible, divine contract. Judgment in Israel was not Areopagus or Agora, it was the Throne of Almighty God. The Prophets saw the scandal of worship offered by people who in daily life were the cause of misery, starvation and pain to the poor of God's People.

Amos is the first "Prophet-Seer" whose messages are recorded in a "Book", although the stories about Nathan at the time of David record the same attitudes. He was speaking before the end of the Northern Kingdom. The first Isaiah saw the same abuses, and the luxury in which the rich people were living. Isaiah 3:16-24 is an astonishing list of the ornaments worn by the women of rich families. Unequal distribution of wealth is absolutely unacceptable to God, and therefore to the Prophet. He is not being "puritanical", his question is "Where does the money come from? How is it acquired?"

Cheating, false weights, inflated prices are universal abuses. Isaiah also saw with horror that the rich were buying land (5:8). Still today, a nomadic culture cannot accept the idea that land "belongs" to any individual person. Land belongs to all. Especially God's Land. So it is that Micah (around 700 B.C.) identifies the evils with city-living, the rich are all there, busy inventing new ways of robbing the poor. He too sees that the Lord will not tolerate this for long, that some kind of judgment must come.

Zephaniah, living at the time of Josiah's belated reforms, sees the almost universal corruption, both social and religious. He begins then to realize that only the poor can really be called "God's People", not because they are poor but because they are not corrupted by wealth and power. Here we find the idea of a Remnant. Disaster may come, but God will remember his Promise and not destroy his People entirely. This distinction between "true Israel" and "socially successful Israel" was to be most important, also for the Gospel and the Church.

To read the Prophets, especially Isaiah and Jeremiah, without this social dimension, would be to understand nothing. They want to see God's will done "on earth as in Heaven" (the Lord's Prayer). "Sin" is what people do to other people, especially when they claim to be religious: "on the day of your fasting, you do as you please and exploit all your workers. Your fasting ends in quarreling and strife, in striking each other with wicked fists... Is not this the kind of fasting I have chosen: to loose the chains of injustice and untie the cords of the yoke, to set the oppressed free and break every yoke? Is it not to share your food with the hungry and to provide the poor wanderers with shelter, when you see the naked, to clothe him?... if you spend yourselves on behalf of the hungry and satisfy the needs of the oppressed, then your light will rise in the darkness, and your night will become like the noonday. The Lord will guide you always" (From Isaiah 58, the "Third Isaiah"). This is the reason why, in Luke 4, Jesus begins his public preaching by quoting Isaiah 61.

【Conclusions】

For Western culture, the Old Testament has always been seen as a preparation for the New Testament; in the Middle Ages it was studied as the early Church had analyzed it, as a collection of "types" anticipating the coming of Jesus, as a preparation for the Gospel. This is mainly because the conflict between Christians and Jews in the early days was so much centered on the meaning of the Old Testament texts. If it is not seen in this way, it may be read as a collection of stories and poems, or as a source book for history and religious studies.

The fundamental dialectic of the Old Testament does not center on such issues as "good and evil", "Heaven and Hell", "Life and Death", or "the individual and society." Israel is always being challenged by the holiness of God, and the Old Testament is unique in viewing human life in this way. The laws of Exodus, Leviticus, Deuteronomy, are partly about worship and partly about social living, but they are all about Holiness. The reason for laws controlling daily life is not order but holiness, God's People must live in the image of their God. Even though certain prophets stress the importance of Justice in society, that too is dictated by the demands of God.

Time in the Old Testament is always historical; if there is a Golden Age, it is not Eden (the stories about Adam and Eve are never mentioned anywhere) but those moments when Israel and God were one, in the Exodus, or in the days of David and Solomon; and it is clear that people were always ready to turn away. The relationship between Man and God shown in the Old Testament is intensely fragile. Because of this, and the passing centuries only stressed it, there came the other, "apocalyptic" dimension. The future "Day of the Lord" became the object of hope, and the source of strength for present struggles.

At the heart of the Old Testament, like the New, is the mystery of human pain. If Job's message is that none can understand it, Isaiah's

Suffering Servant declares that suffering accepted can be socially profitable ("By his wounds we are heated"). Hosea goes even further, seeming to show that God himself suffers.

For the Old Testament is not a work of literature but a complex record of centuries of a nation's life in relationship with the living Lord. It is entirely centered on the conviction that there is a relationship between the people of that nation and the Author of all things, the Lord, God. That relationship is not invented by the people, it is no Myth. It was not even much desired by the people, who kept running away from it. Time after time, in various ways, God returned to his people, inviting them to remember his love for them, his choice of them. The tenderness, the Mercy of God is the theme here, yet even the prophets at times are shown as virtually begging God to go away and leave them in peace. But that too is not possible, if indeed God is the Life of his People.

The Bible: The New Testament

The various books collected in the New Testament represent a very unusual set of data. There is no other moment of ancient history so well documented, no life as fully reported as that of Jesus. Even the Church, after these initial texts (everything in the New Testament was written before A.D. 100), returns to normal near silence for at least a century.

Jesus (the name is really Yeshua, a form of Joshua) wrote nothing, like Socrates. Judging from the silence of the four Gospels, he spent much of his life in unspectacular normality. Then, when he was about 30, he began to speak out, reading the Hebrew Scriptures during the services in the synagogues (Jewish church buildings) so that we may assume that he had studied Hebrew somewhere. He began to travel and teach in the region of Galilee, in the north quite a long way from Jerusalem, where the village people were particularly devout Jews, often living very poor lives rather than mingle with the pagan world. A group of men and women (disciples) formed round him and followed him. Some had been influenced by his cousin John the Baptist who had preached beside the Jordan but had then been imprisoned and executed by Herod Antipas. His execution seems almost to have been the sign for Jesus to start proclaiming in turn that the Kingdom of God was near.

Jesus is shown as a man with no house of his own, of great kindness, which he showed by healing those who were sick and crazy with despair, feeding those who hungered to see God's love. At last, going up to Jerusalem, he was seen as a threat by the powerful religious leaders there. They had him executed by the Romans some three years after he first began teaching in Galilee.

In the Gospels, Jesus is not shown founding a church organization or a new religion. His concern is to renew the Jewish understanding of God and the Law. It is only after his death that the really new declaration comes: "Jesus is Lord, Messiah." His followers, who had called Jesus "Teacher," set out with the message of his Resurrection, saying that he had been seen alive after his death, that his tomb was empty, that he had been taken up into heaven and had sent the Holy Spirit as the sign of God's enduring active presence with them.

The Jews had been looking for a Kingdom, for the coming of the powerful Messianic King shown in Apocalyptic writings. Now Jesus had experienced weakness, failure and death, which was not what the Messiah was expected to do. Yet the "Gospel" (Good News; in Greek and Latin evangelium) arose out of this. The death of Jesus became the supreme victory of God's love. Jesus was the Christ (Greek for Messiah, the Anointed).

Very quickly the first believers found that other people were interested in their message, not only Jews. The whole world seemed full of people thirsting for an encounter between the divine and the human. The Jews had divided the world into Jews and Gentiles, they believed that they had been specially chosen by God. The first Christians realized that this division had been superseded. Jesus had only spoken Aramaic, the first Christians used the international Greek language.

The Letters (often called Epistles) written by Paul are the oldest texts of the New Testament. Paul probably never saw Jesus alive, and when he first heard about the people preaching his resurrection, his reaction was hostile, he helped have them arrested. Paul (at that time called Saul), was a Jewish scholar (Pharisee) from Tarsus who had studied under one of the great teachers of the Law, Gamaliel. On his way to Damascus to attack the Christians there he had a vision, an experience of meeting the Risen Lord who identified himself to him with the words "I am Jesus whom you are persecuting." From that moment, Paul became a believer, and the main messenger of the Good News beyond the Jewish cultural circle.

The Acts of the Apostles, composed by Paul's companion Luke tells mainly his story, of Paul's missionary service leading him ultimately from Jerusalem to Rome, where he was killed. It is remarkable that this main witness to Jesus as Christ had never seen him or heard him teach. The message of Paul, and the other Apostles, was not so much that taught by Jesus in Galilee as the proclamation that in Jesus the whole of humanity was being offered a new relationship with God as their father. A strong sense of universal brotherhood existed in the early community of the Christian church, which was marked by a spirit of sharing and mutual care. From almost the first day, they used the ordinary Greek language. One of their main words was agape, a Greek word meaning love, to which Jesus's life had given a new depth of meaning.

In Latin, Jerome translated this word as caritas (which became in English "charity") which is best expressed by the English "My dear," remembering that something dear can only be had at great expense. The original Latin 'carus, expensive' has just that double meaning.

The other followers of Jesus no doubt also went out preaching the same message, but of their lives we know little or nothing. Even the most important of the Apostles, Simon Peter (his name means Rock; Jesus gave it to him), is only a shadow compared to Paul. Peter could understand that non-Jews might want to believe in Jesus; it was Paul who saw that they did not have to become Jews, that baptism and the fellowship of the Church was enough. Thus while numbers of Jews became Christian Jews, other Jews rejected them and attacked them. Meanwhile, more and more non-Jews found that they wanted to follow the Apostles' teaching about Jesus who had sometimes called himself the Son of Man but who, as Christ, was the Son of God. The word Christian was coined in Antioch as a joke.

The division between Jews and Gentiles underlies many of the letters of Paul, especially the more difficult ones, such as that to the Romans. Paul is having to work out the theory to cover the facts, to see in a new way the relationship between the Jewish Law (expressed in the 'Old' Testament) and the Gospel. The most important word for him in this is freedom, and it sums up his own experience; freedom as opposed to slavery, the holiness that the Old Testament demanded impossibly is now available as a free gift (the original meaning of the word grace) of love offered to all. For Paul as for John, love and life are the same thing, and both have their roots in Christ. Paul's teaching about love is expressed in that most famous chapter 13 of the first letter to the Corinthians, but his concern for the unity of the Christian communities, as well as his intense service of Christ, all are expressions of his vision of love.

The early Christians were in a complex relationship with Time and History. The Resurrection of Jesus was a radical challenge to any idea of continuum, because death is normally the end of an individual's life and here it was not. The Resurrection was seen as a new reality. The Risen Lord would not die again, his body seen with wounded hands and feet when he showed himself to the disciples had not simply "come back to life" for a while. Eternity and time seemed now to coincide.

One possible answer was the Apocalyptic imagery popular among the Jews; this would be the end of the world, all history would soon cease and the Kingdom of God would be revealed to all for ever. This is expressed in the New Testament in the last book, called "Apocalypse" or "Revelations", as well as in certain parts of the Gospels in Jesus's teaching. Paul also seems to expect that the End will soon come.

Only the End did not come, history went on, with children being born and people dying. The Church grew larger and spread across the Roman Empire. The years passed and the old Apostles were killed or died or just disappeared from sight. The city of Jerusalem was captured and destroyed by the Roman general (later emperor) Titus in 70. Several years before this, the Jerusalem Christians had fled the city, as the Jewish rejection of Rome and its culture became increasingly fanatical. There was no longer a Church community in Jerusalem able to point out the places where Jesus had died and been buried. Out of this arose a need for the four texts we call the Gospels, in order to preserve a clear picture of the life of Jesus.

Matthew, Mark, Luke, John, are the names given traditionally to the writers of these four texts. Mark and Luke are both named in Paul's letters and in the Acts of the Apostles as companions of Paul, they were not Apostles, Luke at least was not even a Jew by birth, they had not seen Jesus, probably. Matthew is traditionally identified with Levi, a Jewish tax-gatherer who was called by Jesus and whose life was changed; but it seems unlikely that the person responsible for composing the Gospel bearing his name had ever seen and heard Jesus. It is entirely based on previous written texts and received ideas about him. John is shown as one of the disciples from the earliest days, the brother of James, one of the sons of a fisherman called Zebedee; but it again seems very unlikely that he himself wrote the Gospel bearing his name, although it almost certainly derives from his teaching.

Looking at the texts themselves, we find in each Gospel the same basic structure. At the end of each is a detailed description of the last few days of Jesus's life, his crucifixion and death. This is followed by an evocation of the Resurrection, and is preceded by long chapters telling about his words and deeds during the time of his "active ministry." Each Gospel begins with mention of Jesus's visit to John the Baptist beside the Jordan. At the beginning of each Gospel except Mark there is some kind of prelude, either portraying the birth of Jesus (Matthew, Luke) or outlining the subject of the whole work (John).

The chapters describing Jesus's teaching and actions combine descriptive narratives and "sayings", usually short, even proverbial in style. Very quickly Jesus is seen in conflict with the Jewish religious experts called Doctors, Scribes, Pharisees, who hate him partly because he makes them look foolish in debates.

Comparing the texts in detail, we realize that Matthew, Luke, and Mark have exactly the same words in many places, although sometimes sections are in a different order. Matthew and Luke have many sayings of Jesus not found in Mark, and each of them has narratives and sayings not found anywhere else. But nowhere do we get the impression of an eye-witness changing the other texts because his memory of the actual event was different. Rather the differences show writers reading existing texts, thinking about the idea of Jesus they are trying to express, then adapting the earlier stories and sayings. The Gospels are images of the church's teaching about Jesus as Christ, not biographical memoirs of a long-dead master.

Matthew, Mark and Luke are usually called the "Synoptic Gospels" because they are so close to each other, they agree word-for-word much of the time. The Gospel according to John is very different in its style and contents. Where the Synoptics have brief sayings and anecdotal stories, flashing from one to the other with little linkage, John tells a few stories at length, usually beginning with an action of Jesus which leads into a long explanation of its meaning, or a discussion with the "Jews." Sometimes we find an event related in all four Gospels, such as the Feeding of the Five Thousand, but John gives it deeper meaning by linking it to a great sermon on the Bread of Life. John tells only a few stories where the Synoptics heap up many.

【Matthew】

Long thought to be the first Gospel, the source of the other Synoptics, (but almost certainly in fact depending on Mark) Matthew's Gospel is the longest and the most strongly Jewish of all. It assumes that its readers will know about Jewish customs. It is often similar to Paul in its concerns and vision. It has a clear structure:

1. Infancy Narratives, with the familiar stories of the visit of the Wise Men ("Three Kings") from the East, the Massacre of the Innocents (children of Bethlehem) by Herod, the "Flight into Egypt." These stories are clearly symbolic, each of them based on a passage from the Old Testament which Jesus is found to "fulfill."

2. The Kingdom Appears: Jesus and John the Baptist, the temptations, the first disciples, leading up to the marvelous "Sermon on the Mount" (chapters 5-7) in which Jesus, like a new Moses, proclaims the freedom of the Good News. This begins with the "Beatitudes", (5:1-23), the eight promises that begin "Blessed":

> When Jesus saw the crowds, he went up a mountain and sat down. His disciples came to him, and he began to teach them, saying: "Blessed are the poor in spirit for theirs is the Kingdom of Heaven.

Blessed are those who mourn, for they will be comforted.

Blessed are the meek, for they will inherit the earth.

Blessed are those who hunger and thirst for righteousness, for they will be filled.

Blessed are the merciful for they will be shown mercy.

Blessed are the pure in heart, for they will see God.

Blessed are the peacemakers, for they will be called the children of God.

Blessed are those who are persecuted for righteousness' sake, for theirs is the kingdom of Heaven."

In the Sermon on the Mount, Matthew groups many of the most radically "spiritual" of Jesus' sayings, including the command to "turn the other cheek" (5:39), opposing the rigid Law with a new humanity.

3. The Saving Kingdom: Ten Miracles (chapters 8-9) show Jesus' healing power, then he speaks of his Mission.

4. The Mystery of the Kingdom: There is opposition and division (chapters 11-12), then Jesus speaks in Parables (chapter 13) to express the hidden nature of the Kingdom.

5. The Disciples as the Kingdom: in Matthew (chapters 14-18), the Church is seen as a living Community which is also a living parable of the Kingdom, expressed in sharing and harmony.

6. Judgment: In Matthew, more than any other Gospel, Jesus speaks the language of Apocalypse when faced with the Jewish rejection of his message (chapters 19-25). These chapters are marked with urgency,

not hatred. They are far from soft sentimentality.

7. The Passion (suffering and death) and Resurrection (Chapters 26-28).

【Mark】

For a long time, it was thought that Mark only offered a simplified version of Matthew, with loss of order and no special vision. This is not now accepted. In the twentieth century, with its taste for the fragmented, the rough-hewn, Mark is found more interesting because often more suggestive and open. He also shows considerable doubt about the ability of the disciples to understand and believe in Jesus ("Oh you of little faith!" Jesus keeps exclaiming).

The author of this Gospel is probably the creator of the literary form we call "Gospel"; before him the Church had only collections of "sayings of Jesus" with little or no narrative. In Mark we have detailed descriptions and also explanations of the Jewish background that suggest he was writing for a non-Jewish (gentile) church community. Tradition points to Rome. The whole Gospel is structured on the journey of Jesus towards his suffering and death which are a direct response to his life. Mark, writing for non Jews, does not stress the Christ / Messiah aspect; Jesus is "the Holy One of God" and even "Son of God", as well as the suffering "Son of Man." These terms are easier for ordinary people; yet Mark stresses that Jesus was rejected, not understood, and that he even tried to keep his identity a secret. This may be in part a warning that Jesus's message is not to be understood apart from his death and Resurrection.

The structure of Mark's account of Jesus' life and sayings is quite simple:

1. Jesus makes himself known (chapters 1-8:30) and people respond by faith or rejection; conflict arises although he teaches using parables and performs miracles.

2. Jesus accepts suffering (chapters 8:31-16:8) by turning towards Jerusalem although he "knows" what will happen.

The style of Mark is vivid and sober, he likes to use the word "at once" to imply the dynamic power of the Gospel life. Strangely, the Gospel ends with no story of the disciples meeting with the Risen Lord. What seems to have been the original end at 16:8 leaves the women full of doubt and fear at the message of the angel in the empty tomb. Perhaps a final section was lost at a very early stage? Later writers created a number of extra endings which they added to Mark, using the other Gospels for inspiration.

【Luke】

From the very earliest witnesses we find a clear opinion that this Gospel was written by the "Luke the beloved physician" named by Paul in Colossians 4:14; he is reported to have been a Syrian from Antioch, to have accompanied Paul on his journeys until his death in Rome, after which Luke wrote his Gospel and also the Acts of the Apostles.

Luke was not a Jew, but his Greek style shows how well he knew the Septuagint; he was educated and his Greek is poetic. His Gospel is based on Mark, whom he follows closely, but corrects in many details. The saying of Jesus reported in Luke's chapters 9-18 are not in Mark, the stories and parables found there are also mostly also found in Matthew, but not grouped together there. This extra material that Matthew and Luke seem to have added to Mark in different ways, mostly sayings of Jesus without narrative, is usually called "Q" (German "Quelle" meaning "source").

Luke sets out with a clear vision of his double task: the Gospel traces the journey of Jesus from Galilee to Jerusalem, the "Christ event" culminating in his death and Resurrection. For Luke, this climax in Jerusalem is a turning-point in human history, as it shows God fulfilling his promises "to Abraham and his descendants for ever." While it is an end, it also marks a new beginning. Therefore the second half of Luke's story, the Acts of the Apostles, records the spread of the Gospel from Jerusalem to Rome. Rome is the symbol of "the whole world", Luke's vision of the Risen Christ's presence in ongoing human history is universal.

(1) The Prologue or the Infancy Narratives, (chapters 1-2): telling in parallel the birth of John the Baptist and that of Jesus, with the wonderful events preceding both. Luke is alone in relating the events found in this section, with their rich Old Testament echoes. Mary, the mother of Jesus, plays an essential role, as if Luke had listened to her recollections. She is shown as the ultimate faithful representative or 'remnant' of Israel and at the same time the first believer of the

universal Christian Church, of which she is a symbolic prefiguration.

Luke even includes poetry, modeled in part on Old Testament canticles such as the songs of Moses (Exodus 15) or Hannah (I Samuel 2). Mary , Zechariah, the father of John the Baptist, and Simeon, express the praises of God in lyrics that are still sung by many Christians in their daily worship (songs often still called by their Latin names the"Magnificat" (1:46-55), the "Benedictus" (1:68-79), and the "Nunc dimittis" (2:29-32). It is in Luke that the shepherds hear the story of Jesus's birth from the angels and come to worship in the stable where the child is lying in a manger.

At the end of the section, the 12-year-old Jesus is found by his parents discussing with the teachers in the Temple at Jerusalem; his ministry begins here. The Temple plays a central role in the Prologue: first the birth of John is announced to the unbelieving Zechariah there; then Simeon and Anna welcome the new-born Jesus with songs and prophecy; finally Jesus aged 12 is shown feeling at home there.

(2) The journey : the whole of Luke's Gospel is organized as a journey away from, then back toward, Jerusalem. Jesus grows up and Luke begins the story of Jesus' public ministry with journeys through Galilee (chapters 3 - 9:50). In this section, Luke follows the pattern found in Mark, but removes those aspects of Jesus's words and responses which might confuse educated non Jews, such as his "anger" at the way his disciples are 'slow to believe'.

In Chapter 9 there comes a turning-point. Jesus's words and deeds demand a response of faith; he feeds the 5000 and Peter confesses

"You are the Christ". Jesus is declared to be the Son by the voice speaking from the cloud at his mysterious Transfiguration. Yet on coming down from the mountain Jesus finds his disciples unable to heal a child; his response is to express impatience with the unbelief of the whole generation. Immediately after, he begins to speak of his coming death, which the disciples cannot understand, and in verse 51 Luke says he 'resolutely' set out for Jerusalem, clearly knowing what is to happen there. Faith and rejection are shown to be the two poles of response to his person and his message.

(3) The Pilgrimage: Chapters 9:51-19:27 take us with Jesus from Galilee to Jerusalem. They include all the Q material not in Mark.

(4) The Fulfillment: Chapter 19:28 show Jesus going ahead of his disciples up to Jerusalem, where he 'purifies' the Temple and speaks his final teaching in Chapter 21. These last days of Jesus culminate in the last supper, and the agony in the garden. These are a prelude to his trial, crucifixion and death, which are followed by stories of the his disciples' encounters with the Risen Christ, ending with his Ascension into Heaven, leaving his disciples with the mission to "preach the Good News to the whole world." This is point where the Acts of the Apostles begins. It relates the spread of the Gospel from Jerusalem (Ascension and Pentecost) to Rome.

Luke tells a number of stories not found in the other Gospels. The Infancy Narratives are very different in their style from what follows.

Among the parables of Jesus, that of the Good Samaritan (10:25-37), and that called "the Prodigal Son" (15:11-32), really the parable of "the Forgiving Father," are both only found in Luke, and are the most familiar as well as the most universal of the parables. Among the Resurrection appearances of Jesus, Luke's story of the journey to Emmaus (24:13-35), where the unrecognized Lord instructs two sorrowful disciples, is most meaningful for many. In each of these passages we sense Luke's great narrative skill, his ability to select those details which will speak to all, and his readiness to encapsulate essential Gospel truths in stories developed from perhaps only a vague suggestion in his sources (something we also find in John).

Luke's vision of humanity is central in the social doctrine of the Christian church in the 20th century. In Luke, the Gospel is very clearly intended in a special way for the poor and the weak; the rich are so corrupted and distracted by their wealth, Jesus suggests, that unless they give it away in helping the poor, they will not enter the Kingdom. Jesus in Luke stresses the need for concrete gestures of mercy and kindness in daily life, rather than formal religious obligations. Where Matthew has long passages heralding the Apocalypse, Luke is obviously not at all convinced that the world is about to come to an end. Luke is the evangelist of the active "Christian Life", yet Jesus is shown escaping from the crowds, seeking contemplation in silence and praying in quiet places.

【John】

The most deeply thoughtful of the Gospels, and in its intensity the most poetic, John's Gospel is most remarkable for its use of symbols. John does not follow the style of the Synoptics, with their short, fragmented sayings, although he may have known them. He takes a few actions of Jesus and exploits them to illuminate the nature of Jesus by developing the debates or the preaching which accompany them.

The relationship between the son of Zebedee and the author of this Gospel, traditionally composed at Ephesus, is not clear. The Greek is simple, correct, but the underlying thought is not Greek. John uses words in a very particular way, exploiting their associations to the full. Bread, water, light, life, see, truth, know, believe, love are seemingly universal words, but they are given essentially new meaning by John. Father, Son, Spirit, Word (Logos), I am, glory, commandment, are equally important, and can only be fully understood by readers familiar with the Old Testament.

Indeed, John's Gospel is full of the Old Testament, and John was an Apostle among the Jews, but by the universality of its imagery and message it can be read by all. Yet it demands explanation, more than any other Gospel, and completion by contact with the church community. At the same time, John is the key to deep understanding of the Jesus shown in the other Gospels, he develops and explains things that are only hinted at in them. For example, the relationship between Jesus and God, or the meaning of the feeding of the Five Thousand, or the parallels between Jesus and Moses, or the relationship between the Kingdom of God and this present world. Without John's stress on love in his Gospel and Letters, Christianity might have developed in much more rigid ways.

The structure of John's Gospel is not always clearly articulated:

1. The New Beginning: This opening section begins with a Prologue:
In the beginning was the Word (Logos),
and the Word was with God, and the Word was God.
He was in the beginning with God.
Through him all things were made,
and without him was nothing made that has been made.
In him was life, and the life was the Light of men
The light shines in the darkness,
but the darkness has not comprehended it.
There came a man who was sent from God; his name was John
He came as a witness to testify concerning that Light
so that through him all might believe.
He was not the Light he came to bear witness to the Light;
that was the true Light that lightens every one who comes into the world.
He was in the world,
and the world was made by him,
and the world knew him not;
he came to his own,
and his own received him not.
Yet to all who did receive him,
to those who believed in his name,
he gave power to become children of God;
they were born, not of blood,

nor of the will of the flesh,
nor of the will of a man but of God.
And the Word was made flesh and dwelt among us
and we have seen his Glory,
Glory of the Only Begotten of the Father,
full of grace and truth.

This introduces the witness of John the Baptist (chapter 1), then comes the Marriage at Cana, the 'Beginning of Signs' where there is no more wine, and by the mere presence of Jesus water is changed to wine; the Temple is purified (chapter 2), Jesus baptized by John, the Spirit (chapter 3), the gift of Living Water (chapter 4).

2. The Works of God: Healing (chapter 5), Feeding with the Bread of Life (chapter 6), Light in darkness (chapter 7-8), Sight given to the blind (chapter 9), The Good Shepherd (chapter 10). During this section, the opposition to Jesus grows, "the Jews" reject him.

3. Preparation for Glory: Jesus raises Lazarus, is anointed for death (chapter 11), enters Jerusalem and is eagerly sought for by Greeks, rejected by Jews, he foresees his death (chapter 12).

4. The Hour of Glory: the public works are now finished, Jesus sits down with his friends to eat the Last Supper; he washes their feet (chapter 13), he comforts them by including them in his divine life (chapter 14), he expresses this life in the image of the vine and the

commandment to love one another as he has loved them (chapter 15-16). Then Jesus goes out into the garden and prays, offering his life to God and praying for the unity of all who will believe (chapter 17).

5. The Glory: Jesus is arrested, tried and executed (chapters 18-19); risen from the dead, he is seen by his disciples in ways which confirm his continuing love for them (chapter 20-21).

【The Acts of the Apostles】

In Acts, Luke applies to the early history of the Christian church the same techniques as he had used in his Gospel, telling events in such a way as to bring out their symbolic, inner meaning, and relating them to parts of the Old Testament. Acts is not a simple historical record. It is, however, one of the most remarkable long travel documents of the period, and gives much information about life in the Eastern parts of the Roman Empire.

The starting point is the coming of the Holy Spirit into the church community on the day of the Jewish festival called Pentecost, fifty days after Passover. The uniting force in the Gospel was the person of Jesus, now "taken up" into "heaven"; the unlocated Spirit acts in the same way, guiding the church from within. Historically, Luke was to be proved right in his rejection of imminent eschatology (the end of the age) in favor of on-going history.

For Luke, the first, Jerusalem church community, with its generosity and sharing, its eager gatherings of prayer and fellowship, was the model for others to follow; characteristically, the Jerusalem church (chapters

2 and 4) is very attentive to the needs of the poor.

In the first part of Acts, especially, there are long passages of apostolic preaching. These sermons by Peter, especially, are centered on the proclamation of Jesus as the Messiah in the Jewish context. The Jews either believe or reject this message, culminating in the lynching of Stephen the first martyr (chapter 8) and the mission to Samaria.

In chapter 9, Acts relates the conversion of Paul in dramatic terms and his ministry begins just as, in chapter 10, Peter becomes convinced by a vision that the Gospel is for all mankind, gentiles as well as Jews. In chapter 12, there is suspense when Peter is arrested, and the story of his mysterious release by an angel is full of delightful details.

Chapters 13-14 tell of Paul's first missionary journey, with few clear details. Paul seems to have spent 13 years traveling in the time symbolized by this story. The main point is to show the different problems faced by Paul in preaching to Jews and to pagan gentiles (who are much more open, but more inclined to wrong ideas). This leads to chapter 15, the meeting ("Council") held in Jerusalem at which the "great" apostles Peter and James are seen approving the mission of Paul to the gentiles. Luke does not have room for the great theological debate about the Law found in Paul's letters, he expresses its outcome in this narrative.

Paul then sets out again, in response to a dream, and in chapter 16:10 the narrative suddenly changes into "we", "From Troas we put out to sea and sailed straight for Samothrace." Four times in Acts (here and in chapters 20, 21, 27) descriptions of journeys use this form, implying that the narrator was with Paul. The most vivid moments come in chapter 27, the description of the shipwreck on Malta, one of the most gripping narratives in the New Testament.

In chapter 17, Paul arrives in Athens, and is shown trying rather unsuccessfully to adapt his message to the philosophy majors of the University during his speeches, that to the Areopagus in particular being based on the trial of Socrates. Luke probably realized that Athens, symbolizing Greek culture, was a major symbol for something not yet achieved, the synthesis of the Christian and the philosophical. So too, in chapter 19, there is a symbolic conflict at Ephesus between the Gospel and the old paganism.

From chapter 21, Paul sets out on his journey to death, a structure paralleling Luke's Gospel. Paul is arrested after a riot in the Temple at Jerusalem; as a Roman citizen he demands trial, but the story is told with many speeches in which Paul is shown proclaiming the Gospel, even while he is being lynched. In chapter 25, Paul appeals to Rome, fearing that he will be sent back to Jerusalem and killed. He continues to justify himself, now before the highest authorities he can meet, as a peaceful citizen who hopes for more from Rome than from Jerusalem.

After the episode of the shipwreck (chapter 27), in the last chapter Luke brings Paul to the gates of Rome, accompanied by a crowd of Christians come out to welcome him. His "prison" is a house he rented and he is shown preaching to all. Luke does not mention that during these two years Paul wrote the Letters to the Philippians, to the Ephesians, to the Colossians, and to Philemon. There Luke stops his account. In actual fact, it seems that Paul was released after two years, went to Spain, back to Crete and Greece, and was finally put into a prison in Rome from which he wrote the second Letter to Timothy, sure that his death was near.

[The Epistles of Paul]

Most of the Letters contained in the New Testament are open letters written by Paul to the Christian churches in the cities and areas he had visited: Rome, Corinth (2 letters), Galatia, Ephesus, Philippi, Colossae, Thessalonica (2 letters). Other letters are addressed to individuals: to Timothy (2 letters), Titus and Philemon. They deal with many different questions arising at the time he was writing, some very general, some quite specific to that church or individual. There was no idea that they would be collected together, or that they would still be read every day by Christians 2000 years later.

Within the Epistles, some of the most familiar texts are: Romans chapter 8 (about the relationship of man and Christ by the Spirit), I Corinthians 13 (the "Hymn to Charity"), and 15 (about the Resurrection), Philippians 2:1-11 (on Christ's self-emptying). Ephesians is the most densely poetic of all Paul's writings.

Romans: The main theme of this epistle, written by Paul in Corinth before leaving for Rome in 57-8, is the meaning of "Salvation", the relationship between faith and God's justice, between God and us. In a second section (chapters 12-15), Paul discusses the moral consequences of his ideas. The discovery of salvation as a pure gift of God's grace, and the need for each person to respond by faith, made this the fundamental text for the Reformers of the 16th century, Luther in particular. It is not constructed logically, and is often difficult to read. Especially hard are the passages dealing with the Jewish people.

I Corinthians: This epistle was written because Paul, in Ephesus about 57, had heard of serious conflicts and divisions among the Corinthian Christians. The main themes of the letter are dictated by this situation, Paul discusses the various problems that have arisen, (chapters 1-6), then tries to suggest some solutions, both in detail and in general, as he moves towards a new vision of what the Christian community is (chapters 11-14), and of the hope it lives by because of Christ's Resurrection (chapter 15). The Hymn to Love of chapter 13 is the most well-known part of any Epistle :

If I speak in the tongues of men and of angels, but have not love, I am only a resounding gong or a clanging cymbal. If I have the gift of prophecy and can fathom all mysteries and all knowledge, and if I have a faith that can move mountains, but have not love, I am nothing. If I give all I possess to the poor and surrender my body to the flames, but have not love, I gain nothing. Love is patient love is kind. Love does not envy, it does not boast it is not proud. It is not rude, it is not self-seeking, it is not easily angered, it keeps no record of wrongs. Love does not delight in evil but rejoices with the truth. It always protects, always trusts, always hopes, always perseveres.

Love never fails. But where there are prophecies, they will cease; where there are tongues, they will be stilled; where there is knowledge, it will pass away. For we know in past and we prophesy in part; but when the perfect comes, the imperfect disappears. When I was a child, I talked like a child, I thought like a child, I reasoned like a child. When I became a man I put childish ways behind me. Now we see as in a glass, darkly; but then we shall see face to face. Now I know in part; then I shall fully know, even as I am fully known.

And now these three remain: faith, hope and love. But the greatest of these is love.

II Corinthians: Perhaps the most emotional of all the epistles; Paul is faced with a grave crisis of confidence and he tries to regain the trust of the Corinthians by reminding them of his service in the church, his past history and the past relationships they had. He mentions the needs of the church in Jerusalem, now in great poverty and needing their help, but most of the letter is a personal challenge to enemies who had destroyed his authority. It is intensely personal in tone and tells us much about Paul himself. It reflects the turmoil of journeys, visits, reports, frustrations, delays, that made up Paul's life.

Galatians: It is not clear who these Galatians were; there was a province called Galatia in Asia Minor, but it contained various peoples, not only the Celtic Galatians. The people to whom Paul is writing seem to be gentiles (not Jews) who have become Christians but who have been told by some Jewish Christians that they should observe the Old Testament laws, and be circumcised. The epistle is therefore about the relationship between the Law of Moses and the salvation given by Christ.

This epistle particularly celebrates the freedom which comes with faith in Christ; in style, Paul is following the lessons he learned at school with the Rabbis, and his arguments are not always easy to follow.

Ephesians: Not really a letter at all, but a magnificent theological discourse incorporating many phrases drawn from the young Church's worship, as well as from other letters by Paul. It was almost certainly not originally addressed to the Ephesians, or any particular church. It is often said that Paul may not be the author. The main sections of the text are prayer (chapters 1-3) and exhortation (chapters 4-6); the first part especially offers a vision of the Christian "mystery" that represents a vital step in the development of the doctrine of the Trinity (God is one, yet the unity is a fellowship of love involving Father, Son and Spirit). Unity is also the moral theme of the epistle, human unity linked to the establishment of Christ's kingdom.

Philippians: Probably written at Rome in 61-3, while Paul was in prison. The main theme of the epistle, written to Macedonian Christians, is joy and fellowship. Fellowship (Greek koinonia) is relationship with God and with other Christians, and joy is the result of union with Christ's suffering and Resurrection. The hymn to Christ in chapter 2:5-11 is particularly impressive. It sums up the nature of Christ's coming into the world as a "self-emptying", as it struggles with the paradox of his humiliation and his glory:

Let that mind be in you which was in Christ Jesus,

Who, being in very nature God,
did not consider equality with God something to be grasped,
but made himself nothing, taking the very nature of a servant,
being made in human likeness.
And being found in appearance as a man,
he humbled himself and became obedient to death
even death on a cross!
Therefore God exalted him to the highest place
and gave him the name that is above every name,
that at the name of Jesus every knee should bow,
in heaven and on earth and under the earth,
and every tongue confess that Jesus Christ is Lord,

【Other books】

At the end of the New Testament are a number of letters attributed to Peter, and to John, and the final book known as the Revelation is also attributed to John. It is the most difficult book of the bible, full of difficult symbolism, as it attempts to suggest how the final victory of the love of God will come about.

The Early Christian Church

Almost all of the information we have on the early years of the Church comes from the New Testament. The Letters of Paul and the other apostles are the earliest documents of the New Testament, and from them we can deduce the main features of the early church. The other parts of the New Testament, Gospels, the Acts of the Apostles, Revelation were written in their present form at a time when the first generation of "eye-witnesses" was disappearing. The Acts of the Apostles is our main source for historical information about this period.

The first Christians were, like Jesus, Jews, and like Jesus they experienced opposition and "persecution" from the Jewish leaders. The early deaths of Christian "martyrs" (witnesses) recorded in Acts are the result of this conflict (Stephen, James). From the beginning the church actively spread its message, while the Jews felt that as the Chosen People, they had above all to keep themselves apart from the "gentiles" (other nations). The Jews were a recognized nation within the Empire, their religion was that of an allied people, but not liked because of its exclusivity.

Christianity first found non-Jewish members among those who, tired of the official Roman religion, were interested in the monotheistic, historical faith of the Jews. The anti-legalistic teaching of Jesus ("Love one another"), the element of mystery offered by the proclamation of his Resurrection from the dead, the promise of salvation after death in his coming Kingdom, all had great appeal for such searchers after God. Where the Jews had demanded that those sharing their faith should be circumcised and keep all their complicated traditions and laws, the Christians only asked them to receive Baptism and believe in the faith taught by the Apostles, expressed in what is still called the Apostles' Creed:

> I believe in God the Father almighty
> maker of heaven and earth,
> and in Jesus Christ his only Son, our Lord,
> who was conceived by the Holy Spirit,
> born of the Virgin Mary,
> suffered under Pontius Pilate,
> was crucified, died and was buried,
> he descended into Hell,
> the third day he rose again from the dead,
> he ascended into heaven
> and is seated at the right hand of God, the Father almighty;
> He will come to judge the living and the dead,
> and his kingdom will have no end;
> I believe in the Holy Spirit,
> the holy, catholic Church,
> the communion of saints,
> the forgiveness of sins,

the resurrection of the body,
and the life everlasting.

In each place there must have been varying traditions but it seems that everywhere the Church's main celebration took place in the night between Saturday and Sunday. In each local assembly (ekklesia) there was normally one episkopos (president of a council, giving the English "bishop") and a council of elders (Greek presbyteroi, from which comes the word "priest"). There were also diakonoi, deacons who serve the needs of the community in concrete ways, especially helping those who are poor or sick (the Greek root of "deacon" means "serve", as also that of the Latin "minister"). Some communities were certainly more democratic than others, and the bishops of Churches that had memories of having been founded by Paul or another of the Apostles felt particular responsibility for maintaining the purity of the Apostolic teaching.

Very quickly, there were groups of Christians in all the main cities of the Roman Empire. When Paul arrived in Rome for his trial he was welcomed by members of the church there. The Greek and Latin word for "church", ecclesia, is that used for the Assembly in Greek democracy, and for great gatherings of Israel as God's People in the Greek Old Testament, the Septuagint. From the beginning, there were people of every class, rich and poor, present at the worship and meetings of the church, offering possibilities for sharing wealth or for tensions. The Gospel spread amazingly rapidly, thanks in part to the ease of communications offered by the Empire's almost universal Greek.

[Persecutions and Martyrdom]

Many people imagine that in the early centuries, Christians were always being fiercely persecuted. This is far from the truth. Except for the drama of Nero's accusation against the Christians after the fire of Rome in 64, Rome did not actively persecute the Christians. They were seen as part of the wider 'Jewish problem' and not something separate. Only later, as the number of Christians grew, and the ceremonies celebrating the living emperor as a god were developed, did conflict arise. It may be that in the East, where there were many Jews, they were able to make trouble for the Christians with the authorities, but this was not general. Thus Trajan, in his reply to Pliny's letter asking how Christians should be treated, told him that although the Christian religion was illegal (perhaps because it was "secret" and individual), he should not search for Christians, but act if one was accused directly (the accuser had to direct the prosecution and was punished if the case was found not proved).

The first century of the church's history is almost unknown to us apart from the New Testament. Sudden outbursts of persecution leave their mark in stories about heroic martyrs. In 155(?), in Smyrna (now Turkey) the 86 year-old bishop Polycarp (who was John's disciple) was seized and burned, although he was much respected in the city. In Lyons (France) in 177 a mob forced the martyrdom of 48 Christians, including the brave young slave Blandine. At this time, many people believed terrible rumors about the Christians' practices. They were said to murder children, eat human flesh, commit incest. Persecution was usually a result of some kind of mob-hysteria, not an official policy. Christians had by now begun to try to communicate their beliefs to educated Roman citizens, not merely to communicate faith, but also to explain that they were loyal citizens of the Empire and not rebels. By 180, we find many Christian groups in North Africa, where the church became for the first time Latin-speaking, Until then, even in Rome, it had mostly used Greek.

The first official, empire-wide persecution only came in 202, under Septimus Severus; it was launched for no clear reason, and there were martyrs in Alexandria, Rome, Corinth, and Carthage. From Carthage we have a document recording the suffering of two young women, the high-class Perpetua and the slave Felicity, partly written as a diary by Perpetua herself, which is most moving. She was hardly more than twenty, married and had a small child.

It is not surprising that many of the onlookers at such scenes came away convinced that the martyrs' faith must be true. Many must have repeated the words heard when old Polycarp had insisted that he alone should be killed: "Look how much these Christians love one another; they are even ready to die for each other."

Those who were killed professing faith in God were thought to have died like Jesus, and so they began to be called 'martyrs' (witnesses) and 'saints' (holy people) although Paul had used the word 'saint' to describe every Christian who had been baptized. People began to venerate the bodies and tombs of the saints, as well as cloths dipped in their blood. Catechumens who were killed before baptism were said to have undergone a 'baptism of blood'. Believers who were imprisoned and tortured but not killed were often referred to as 'Confessors' and treated with special veneration after their release. In Rome, many martyrs were buried in the Catacombs, the underground corridors lined with tombs that were a popular place of burial.

This persecution ceased, but in 212 the emperor Caracalla granted Roman citizenship to almost all the free inhabitants of the lands in the empire. Now, Roman citizens were obliged to acknowledge the gods of the empire, and to make the offerings of the cult of the emperor as god. For a time, this problem was not acute, and it is in these years that Christians first built special buildings for their worship in Asia Minor.

【Early Christian Thinkers】

At this time, office in the church was becoming socially desirable, many new converts were coming for instruction and baptism, and new thinkers were arising. Irenaeus, a pupil of Polycarp, and bishop of Lyons after the martyrdom of 177 until his death in 202, wrote a number of theological works, especially a defence of Christianity against the Gnostic heresy. He is sometimes called the "first systematic theologian." His most celebrated saying is: "The glory of God is Man alive."

Origen (185-255) is perhaps the first major Christian intellectual, although much of what he wrote is now lost. He was born and lived in Alexandria, where his father was martyred in 202. He became head of the Catechetical School but was later (231) obliged to settle in Palestine. During the great persecution under Decius (250) he was tortured and he died soon afterwards. He was a controversial figure because of the originality of his thought. He was interested in the textual criticism of the Bible, and wrote commentaries on the Scriptures. a presentation of basic Christianity, an apology for Christianity (Contra Celsum) in reply to an earlier pagan attack. He was highly esteemed by the writers who followed him, such as Gregory of Nazianzus, Basil, and Eusebius.

Quite unlike him, while living at the same time, was Tertullian of Carthage (160-240). He was born into the old world, attracted by the rigors of Stoicism, then became a Christian attracted by the purity of life and the spirit of the martyrs. He was a lawyer by training, a rhetorician, and his many writings in Latin are a brilliant expression of the most "puritanical" form of non-conformist Christianity. He was by nature an extremist, he joined the most radical groups, expecting the destruction of the evil world at any moment, he resisted any compromise with the pagan world and its culture. The West received much of its thought on politics and religion from him.

【Persecutions and Victory】

In 250, at a time when the Empire was threatened with Germanic invasion, the emperor Decius called on all citizens to sacrifice to the gods. Those unable to produce a certificate proving that they had offered the sacrifice would be punished. In the cities, the Christians were unprepared for this, and many chose to make the sacrifice, which made them guilty of apostasy. Much worse was to come. The next emperor, Valerian, from 257-9 set out to suppress Christianity and enforce the cult of the Roman gods. This was the worst of all the persecutions in the West, many died, perhaps the emperor was tempted by the wealth of the church, which was already considerable.

The final struggle came in 303, when Diocletian ordered the

destruction of church buildings, the confiscation of the Scriptures, and pagan sacrifice by the clergy. In 304 he even demanded a universal sacrifice. He realized that now Christianity had spread from the cities to the countrysides, into Armenia and Persia, and was a real threat to the old religion. He felt that the present problems of the Empire came from neglect of gods like Jupiter and Hercules, and the presence of "foreign" religions seemed likely to displease them more. However, he ordered that people were not to be killed, and in 305 he abdicated.

It was only now that the word 'pagan' begins to be used to describe people who follow non-Christian religions. The word originally meant 'rural' and serves to remind us that Christianity spread much more quickly among the urban population of the Empire. 'Paganism' remained strong in the rural areas for many centuries, until it slowly declined into 'superstition' or 'popular religion' and ceased to be felt to be threatening.

In the East, anti-Christian activities continued for a few more years while Constantine was struggling against his rival Maximinus. The final triumph of Christianity came about in strange ways. Constantine believed like many Romans of his time that the sun was the one true God. This cult of the sun was widespread, with the resulting confusion between the physical sun and its symbolic uses; Christians still worship on Sundays. Constantine told Eusebius that he once had a vision of a cross combined with the sun, with the message 'In this sign, conquer.' In 312, when Maximinus could have stayed safely inside the walls of Rome, he suddenly emerged and was defeated at the Milvian Bridge across the Tiber by Constantine's much smaller army. This 'God-given' victory was decisive in Constantine's conversion to faith in Christ as the true Sun of Justice.

Soon after it, he was instructed in a dream to use the 'Chi-Ro' symbol of Christ on his standards and coins as a sign of victory.

The outcome of this process was Constantine's Edict of Milan (313), which is more than a simple declaration of tolerance for Christianity; it marks the beginning of the process by which orthodox, catholic Christianity became the official religion of the Roman Empire under The who in 391 ordered the final closing of all temples and the abolition of pagan worship.

【The Teaching Church】

After Origen, the most important name is that of Eusebius (260-340), who became bishop of Caesarea, in his native Palestine, in 314. Origen had lived his years of exile there and Eusebius admired him very much, most of what we know about Origen comes from him. Eusebius was close to Constantine, whom he admired. His vision and writings are mostly historical, his vision of history is of a conquest of Christian, biblical truth over pagan ideas. His Alexandrian education, though, meant that he respected the achievements of the ancient world, seeing in them a providential Praeparatio Evangelica (preparation for the Gospel, the name of a work in which he shows how even the best Greek philosophy, that of Plato, is equaled by the Bible). His main fame rests on his Ecclesiastical History, inspired by classical history, which traces the history of the church from its beginnings until 324. Eusebius is the model for all later Western ecclesiastical historians (Bede, for example), by his direct quotation of ancient records and authorities.

Eusebius reflects the basic problem of the relationship within

Christianity of the two cultures, biblical and classical. Within the church, however, there were other problems. The gravest of these were those forms of teaching called Arianism and Donatism. This latter divided the North African church after the Great Persecution (303-5) when some had surrendered copies of the Scriptures to the authorities (traditores, meaning 'surrenderers', from which the word "traitors"). Later, the extremists in the church refused to accept these people as members of the church, so that in the time of Augustine we find two parallel churches, the Catholic (ready to forgive) and the Donatist (strict, unforgiving followers of the bishop Donatus).

Arianism, though, was an Eastern problem, Alexandrian in origin. Arius was a priest in Alexandria, and in talking of God he seems to have said that the Son, Christ, since he suffered and died, was obviously "inferior" to the Father who is above all that. At the beginning of the preaching of the Gospel, Christians had been challenged by Gnostics who had said that Jesus, being God, could not have been a "real" man. Now they were challenged by the idea that, being a man, Jesus could not "really" be God. Since the church has always wanted to stress that the Gospel is one of reconciliation between God and Man in Christ, ideas which deny one side of the equation matter. Yet the ideas taught by Arius seemed right to many, they spread by missionaries as far as the Germanic Goths who were later going to invade Italy.

Constantine wanted unity among the Christians, so in 325 over 200 bishops met in Nicaea (Turkey) with Constantine presiding to "settle" the problem. The result, eventually, was the "creed" that is called the Nicene Creed, declaring that the Son is "of one substance with the

Father." This is the Credo sung in Masses by Bach, Mozart, Beethoven etc. It did not settle the problem, but with time Arianism melted away.

【Ambrose and Augustine】

The next important name is that of Ambrose (339-397) who was chosen to be bishop of Milan (Italy) before even he had been baptized. Before this he had been a local governor. He exerted great influence over emperors, especially Theodosius, with the aim of having a single, unified church uniting every person in the Empire. He was therefore opposed to "heretical" groups (Arians, Donatists etc.), to pagan religions, and to the Jews. He was outraged when the "Christian" Theodosius in 390 had 7,000 citizens of Thessalonica massacred in a theater; he excluded him from the church and made him do penance. In writing and preaching, he drew on deep knowledge of Platonic philosophy, his sermons helped to convert Augustine, who was moved to tears by his hymns.

Augustine (354-430) is the greatest figure in the transition from classical to medieval (and modern) culture. He was born in what is now Algeria and his mother, Monica, was a devout catholic Christian. He received a classical education and at 19, reading Cicero, discovered the possible depths of philosophy. He therefore turned away from the Christianity of his mother and began a spiritual pilgrimage in search of Wisdom which led him to Manichaeism.

He began to teach rhetoric, teaching at Carthage, Rome and Milan. At Milan he was attracted by the Christianized Neo-Platonism of Ambrose, for his was a tormented psyche, intensely aware of the tensions and contradictions between the visible and the invisible, nature and Grace. In his Confessions, he tells how he was reading the Bible one day, when he found in Paul's Letter to the Romans a key to his distress and realized that he had become a Christian. He was baptized at Easter 387, to the great joy of his mother. She died suddenly of a fever in the autumn, as they were on the way back to Africa.

Returning to North Africa, he set up a kind of monastic community; in 391 he became a priest, against his will, and in 395 he became bishop of the town of Hippo where he served for 34 years. His mind was intensely active, he wrote many works designed to support the catholic doctrines against other groups (Donatists) and against the Gnostic Manichees. He left over 100 works, 200 letters, 500 sermons. The most famous of his works are the Confessions and The City of God. The Confessions (c.400)tell the story of his early struggles, his conversion and new life, in a vivid, emotional way. Intensely "personal" in a way nothing written before it had been, it is one of the great classics of spiritual autobiography. In many ways, Augustine invented "modern man" by the depiction of his inner struggles, contradictions, and doubts in the Confessions.

In 410, Rome fell to the Goths, and for Augustine this seemed a sign of the end of the world, since Rome was for him the symbol of all civilized culture. So he began to write a book! The *City of God*(413-426) is the basic work in which Christianity and classical culture are united, thanks to Augustine's vision. This vision is literary in its use of language, Neo-Platonic in its fundamental approach, biblical in its teaching. Almost certainly, no book has marked Western culture so deeply. Yet Augustine is no easy writer, and his ascetic doctrine, his distrust of the physical world (he was deeply tempted by ambition as well as sensuality), his doctrine of the deep depravity of fallen humanity redeemed only by God's saving Grace, underlie the deep pessimism of what is often called Western Puritanism. Calvinism in particular was deeply influenced by his dualistic vision.

Because of Augustine's writings, the Middle Ages and the Renaissance were essentially Neo-Platonic, without realizing it. Until the Renaissance almost none of Plato's works existed in Latin translation and they were not read in the West. Protestant theology remains deeply marked by his influence, in its doctrines of Grace, its concern with (double) predestination, its "other-worldliness", and its love of verbal discourse.

The other great name of these years is that of Jerome (348-420) who was more of a pure scholar than Augustine, who was an intellectual and a pastor. His character was even more complicated than that of Augustine; he found human relations very difficult. His teacher, Aelius Donatus, was the most famous "grammarian" of the age, he wrote two school books on grammar and rhetoric that were used throughout the Middle Ages. Jerome was baptized when he was a student and then went to the Syrian desert and learned Hebrew. He met the great teacher Gregory of Nazianzus in Constantinople, then returned to Rome, where he revised the style of the Latin New Testament then in use.

In 385, he left Rome and traveled to Syria and Egypt to see the monastic communities living there, before settling for the rest of his life in Bethlehem with a community of Roman followers, men and women. There he completed the new translation of the Old Testament into Latin, based on the work of Origen, that became the official Latin Bible until the present age, known as the Vulgate. Jerome's style is the most classical of all the Christian writers, full of echoes of Cicero, Virgil, Horace.

【Into the Middle Ages】

With the fall of Rome and the collapse of the Empire in the West, the "Dark Ages" came to Britain and Gaul. A number of writers were vital for the transmission of classical values. Orosius came from Spain to be with Augustine and at his suggestion wrote a Christian chronicle history of the world from its foundation, through the Roman empire, until the present (417), using Eusebius' and Jerome's works, and pagan histories. It was the basic work of history for the Middle Ages.

Macrobius (c.420), an otherwise unknown African officiallll, left two works which the Middle Ages built on: his neo-platonic Commentary on Cicero's Somnium Scipionis (the "Dream of Scipio") by which medieval dream-visions and other dream literature were inspired; and his Saturnalia ("New Year's Party") which is a kind of didactic symposium centered on the meaning and importance of Virgil as the model Rhetorician, but covering many topics. In the Middle Ages it served as a kind of encyclopedia.

Another North African, Martianus Capella (c.410-430), composed a didactic treatise combining prose and verse (Menippean Satire), the "Marriage of Mercury and Philology" in which a personified Philology goes on a journey to heaven with her servants, the Seven Liberal Arts, to be married to Mercury who is god of Eloquence. It gave the idea of the heavenly-ascent allegory to the Middle Ages, and also the outline of the basic course of education in Grammar Schools and Universities until the 19th century: the Trivium of Grammar, Logic (or Dialectic), Rhetoric, after which a student became Bachelor of Arts (B.A.), and the Quadrivium of Geometry, Arithmetic, Astronomy, Music, after which he became fit to teach others, as Master of Arts (M.A.) or went on to study Philosophy and Theology.

The other writer by whom the classics were transmitted to the West is Boethius (480-524). He was of a noble Roman family, and served as consul in 510. His was the last generation to be able to study the Greek classics in Greek, and one of his goals was to translate the works of Aristotle and Plato into Latin, with commentaries reconciling the differences between them. If he had succeeded, Western intellectual history would be different, there would have been no rediscovery of Aristotle in the 12-13th centuries, no ignorance of Plato in the Middle Ages, no rediscovery of him in the 15th century! But after having served under Theodoric the Ostrogoth, he was suspected of treason, put in prison, and finally executed.

While in prison, Boethius wrote his immensely influential *Consolation of Philosophy*, a mixture of prose and verse, a dialogue in which the personified figure of Philosophy explains to him how philosophy enables him to live truly as a human being even in absurd and cruel situations such as his. The fundamental question explored in this book is the nature of true happiness.

The work alternates sections in verse with the prose debate between Boethius (who takes the role of the blockhead who needs always to be instructed) and Philosophy. In Book 1 Boethius expresses his anguish in verse, to which Philosophy replies in prose. He contrasts the harmonious order of Nature with the apparent disorder of human life in which people suffer for no just reason. Initially, Boethius thinks that everything is the work of Fortune, a personification of blind destiny, who turns the wheel that raises people to prosperity or plunges them into disaster. In which case there is no meaning and no justice in life.

In Book 3, Philosophy prays to God in a much-admired Platonic hymn, before showing Boethius that God is the perfect Good which can alone be the source of true happiness. God here is the Platonic Good rather than the Christian God, but Boethius stresses the omnipotent Providence that ensures that human lives are not unjustly subject to mere chance.

The work ends with a long discussion about the nature of Providence and the possibility of human freedom when everything is already known to God's eternal mind. The themes of the work are classical commonplaces, and the work is above all remarkable for its self-restraint; for although Boethius was certainly a Christian, he nowhere uses faith as an easy escape from difficult questions. He always refers to the possibilities available to the philosophical mind, whether Christian or not.

King Alfred, Chaucer, and Queen Elizabeth, are among those who translated the Consolation into English. It was one of the most important works of "practical philosophy" in the Middle Ages, when many people were always struggling to understand the workings of "Fortune"and Providence in life.

Less familiar, but just as important, Cassiodorus (490-583) should be better known. He followed Boethius as consul and in other offices, then retired, after failing to create a Christian university in Rome. He spent at least 10 years in Constantinople, then returned and created a monastery on his land in Calabria (Italy), the Vivarium. The most important feature of this monastery, created at about the time when Benedict was founding the first Benedictine monasteries at Subiaco and Monte Cassino, is its stress on the intellectual activities of the monks. The Vivarium is above all vital for Western civilization by its library. Other monasteries, like that founded in North England in the following century by Benedict Biscop, followed its example, and these monastic libraries, hidden in remote areas, preserved the classical manuscripts that played a vital role in the moments of "Renaissance": that led by the monk Alcuin under Charlemagne, that of the 12th century (Abelard) which saw the founding of the modern universities, that of the 14th century led by Petrarch, that of the 16th century led by Erasmus. Cassiodorus also organized the translation of various Greek works into Latin.

The link between the scientific learning of Antiquity and its rediscovery in the high Middle Ages is very often Isidore of Seville (620-636), a bishop who wrote books about history, science, theology, but whose most important work was the Etymologiae or "Origins", an encyclopedia in the tradition of similar works by Boethius and Cassiodorus, in which he notes briefly everything he thinks worth knowing about everything.

Finally, Prudentius (348-405) was the writer of great Latin hymns and, most important, of the allegorical epic the Psychomachia (the battle of the soul) from which all medieval allegories and Morality plays derive, thanks to its portrayal of the soul torn between the forces of Good and Evil represented by personified Virtues and Vices, good and bad angels.

Major Dates

2560 B.C. Cheops of Egypt dies (Great Pyramid).

1500 Minoan culture in Crete.

1350 Tutankhamen.

1250 Ramses II of Egypt; Moses.

1200 Destruction of Troy.

1012 David becomes King.

972-931 King Solomon; Jerusalem Temple built.

800-700 Homer.

750-700 Greeks adopt alphabet.

722 Destruction of Northern Kingdom of Israel (Samaria).

700 Hesiod.

600-500 Zoroaster, Confucius, Buddha, Pythagoras, Lao Tzu, Second Isaiah, Jeremiah, Parmenides, Heraclitus...

587 Nebuchadrezzar takes Jerusalem Jewish Exile in Babylon.

536 Jews return to Jerusalem.

490 Battle of Marathon.

480 Persian invasion; Thermopylae; Athens burnt; Salamis.

500-420 Anacreon, Pindar, Parmenides & Zeno, Phidias, Herodotus.

470-400 Aeschylus, Sophocles, Euripides, Aristophanes.

460-429 "Age of Pericles" in Athens.

437 Parthenon dedicated.

404 Athens surrenders to Sparta.

403 Popular uprising restores Democracy in Athens.

399 Trial and Death of Socrates.

347 Death of Plato.

322 Death of Aristotle.

336-323 Alexander the Great conquers Middle East, reaches India.

323 Death of Alexander in Babylon.

323 Ptolemy family begins to rule Egypt from Alexandria.

264-227 Asoka first King of united India, Buddhist art begins.

218-203 Hannibal (from Carthage) in Italy.

200-160 Plautus (d. 184), Terence (d. 159).

146 Romans destroy Carthage; Roman Empire begins to grow.

100-44 Cicero, Marius, Cato, Sulla, Pompey, Crassus, Julius Caesar.

55 Julius Caesar first lands in Britain.

44 Julius Caesar killed in Senate by Brutus, Cassius.

31 Battle of Actium; deaths of Antony and Cleopatra.

27 Octavian given title "Augustus."

27-A.D.14 The Augustan Age: Virgil, Horace, Ovid.

5 / 4 B.C. Jesus born.

A.D. 33? Jesus crucified; Resurrection proclaimed; Church begins.

54-68 Nero.

64 Fire of Rome; Peter and Paul martyred.

65 Seneca ordered to commit suicide.

65-90 Gospels written.

70 Titus captures Jerusalem, destroys it. Jewish "Diaspora" complete.

212 Persecution of Christians intensifies.

284-305 Diocletian Emperor; final persecution.

306-337 Constantine the Great.

313 Edict of Milan, Christianity accepted.

325 Council of Nicea; Arianism rejected.

331 Constantinople becomes main capital of Empire.

374-397 Ambrose, of Milan, influences Augustine

387 Augustine baptized; Bishop of Hippo 396-430.

381-395 Theodosius makes Christianity the state religion.

404 Legions leave Britain.

410 Alaric (Visigoth) captures Rome.

453 Attila the Hun sacks Rome, dies.

800 Charlemagne crowned Holy Roman Emperor.

· index